2⁻

SCHOTT'S ORIGINAL
MISCELLANY

SCHOTT'S ORIGINAL
MISCELLANY

Conceived, written, and designed by

BEN SCHOTT

BLOOMSBURY

Schott's Original Miscellany™

Copyright © BEN SCHOTT 2002

Published by Bloomsbury, New York and London
Distributed to the trade by Holtzbrinck Publishers

www.miscellanies.info

First US Edition 2003

3 5 7 9 10 8 6 4

The above numbers (sometimes referred to as 'reprint' or 'strikeout' numbers)
provide information on the print run of a book: the lowest number visible
shows the run from which the book originated.

Cover illustration © Alison Lang 2002
Illustrations on p14 & p87 are from *Open Here* (Thames & Hudson)
by kind permission of the authors, P. Mijksennar & P. Westendorp.

Library of Congress Cataloging-in-Publication Data has been applied for.

ISBN is the International Standard Book Number. It is always a ten-digit code, and
while it is not essential for a published book to have an ISBN, the number is widely
used by booksellers, libraries, publishers, and distributors for cataloguing and stock
control. The ten digits are divided into four sections, separated by hyphens or spaces.
The first section identifies the national, geographical, or linguistic grouping of the
publisher; the second identifies the name of the publisher; the third identifies the title
or edition; and the fourth is a check-digit used to mathematically validate the ISBN.

ISBN 1-58234-349-7

Designed & typeset by BEN SCHOTT
Printed in the United States of America by
R.R. Donnelley & Sons Company, Crawfordsville, Indiana

SCHOTT'S ORIGINAL MISCELLANY

An encyclopedia? A dictionary? An almanac? An anthology? A lexicon?
A treasury? A commonplace? An amphigouri? A vade-mecum?

Well… yes. *Schott's Original Miscellany* is all of these and, of course, more.

Schott's Original Miscellany is a snapper-up of unconsidered trifles. Its purpose is to gather the flotsam and jetsam of the conversational tide. Importantly, *Schott's Original Miscellany* makes very few claims to be exhaustive, authoritative, or even practical. It does, however, claim to be essential. It is, perhaps, possible to live one's life without *Schott's Original Miscellany*, but it seems a curious and brave thing to attempt.

> MISCELLANY [mis.sel.iny] *noun* 1: A collection, medley, or mixture. 2: A collection of papers or treaties on a particular subject. 3: A volume or publication containing miscellaneous information of general interest on a variety of subjects. [OED]

───────────── TO FORGIVE, DIVINE ─────────────

Painstaking efforts have been made to ensure that all of the information contained within the *Miscellany* is correct. But, as Alexander Pope noted, 'to err is human'. Consequently, the author can accept no responsibility if you play a losing hand in poker; fail to be granted Executive Clemency; get lost on Hollywood Boulevard; order a disagreeable sort of sushi; shrink all of your socks; or say something utterly come-hither in Swedish.

Many of the facts within the book are the subject of debate and dispute. A brief discussion of just a few such disputations can be found on p153.

If you have suggestions[†], corrections, clarifications, or questions, please email them to usa@miscellanies.info – or send them to the author care of: Bloomsbury Publishing, 175 Fifth Avenue, New York, N.Y. 10010, USA.

[†] The author reserves the right to treat any and all suggestions as his own, and to use them in future editions, other related or unrelated projects, or simply to add color to his conversation.

THE FOLLOWING PEOPLE deserve their share of the blame:

Jonathan, Judith, and Geoffrey Schott.

Clare Algar, Louisa Allen, Stephen Aucutt, Joanna Begent,
Dan Berkowitz, Esther Berkowitz, Paul Binski, Martin Birchall,
James Brabazon, John Casey, Robbie Clemovich, James Coleman,
Martin Colyer, Victoria Cook, Aster Crawshaw, Rosemary Davidson,
Jody Davies, Colin Dickerman, Jennifer Epworth, Penny Gillinson,
Gaynor Hall, Elinor Hodgson, Julian Hodgson, Miriam Hodgson,
Max Jones, Hugo de Klee, Alison Lang, Rachel Law, John Lloyd,
Jess Manson, Michael Manson, Susannah McFarlane, Charles Miller,
Polly Napper, Sarah Norton, Cally Poplak, Dena Rosenberg,
Daniel Rosenthal, Tom Rosenthal, Paul Sweeney, Greg Villepique,
Ann Warnford-Davis, and William Webb.

To them my thanks are due for suggestions, advice, encouragement,
expert opinions, and other such things. If glaring errors exist within this
book, it's probably their fault.

'Let us not take it for granted that life exists

more fully in what is commonly thought big

than in what is commonly thought small.'

— VIRGINIA WOOLF

GOLF STROKE NOMENCLATURE

Double Bogey	+2	-1	Birdie
Bogey	+1	-2	Eagle
Par	0	-3	Albatross, Double Eagle

HAT TAX

Between 1784 and 1811, the British government levied a tax on the sale of hats. A graduated scale existed, ranging from $3d$ [on hats costing less than $4s$], to $2s$ [for hats costing more than $12s$]. Purveyors of hats were obliged to purchase a Licence [£2 in London, $5s$ outside], and to display a sign proclaiming them a *Dealer in Hats by Retail*. To enforce this tax, duty-stamps were printed which had to be pasted into the lining of every hat. Evasion of the Hat Tax, by retailer or hat-wearer, was punishable by a fine; forgery of hat-duty stamps was ultimately punishable by death. For some curious reason, the tax applied only to men's hats. Similar taxes of the time included: Glove Tax (1785–94); Almanac Tax (1711–1834); Dice Duty (1711–1862); Hair-Powder Tax (1786–1869); Perfume Tax (1786–1800); and Wallpaper Tax (1712–1836). Perhaps the best-known duty of this type is Window Tax, levied first in 1697 to replace revenue lost through coin clipping. Initially, nearly every house was charged $2s$; properties with 10–20 windows paid $4s$; and those with more than 20 windows paid $8s$. These charges soon escalated, and consequently the practice of 'stopping up' became common. Windows were exempt from the count if they were permanently filled with materials matching the adjacent walls. Inspectors would regularly count exposed windows and ensure any stopped windows had not 'broken out'. Over time, the tax grew more unpopular, and it deprived residents (especially those in already disadvantaged areas) of daylight. In 1851 the tax was abolished.   [Currency: s = Shilling · d = Penny]

CHARACTERISTICS OF LIVING THINGS

Movement · Respiration · Sensitivity · Growth · Reproduction
Excretion · Nutrition · [useful acronym: MRS GREN]

SHOELACE LENGTH

Pairs of holes	length (cm)		
2	45	5	75
3	45 *or* 60	6	90 *or* 110
4	60	8	150
		9	180

CRICKETING DISMISSALS

Hit Wicket · Caught · Bowled · Run Out · Handled Ball · Stumped
Hit Ball Twice · Timed Out · Leg Before Wicket · Obstructed Field

NOUNS OF ASSEMBLAGE

a malapertness of peddlers
a spring of teals
a gang of elk
a murmuration of starlings
a suit of sails
a wilderness of monkeys
a doping of sheldrake
a clutch of eggs
a coven of witches
a staff of servants
a field of runners
a sheaf of arrows
a chattering of choughs
a cete of badgers
a bench of bishops
a murder of crows
a bundle of rags
a barren of mules

a pontification of priests
a rag of colts
a walk of snipe
an exaltation of larks
a muster of peacocks
a desert of lapwing
a drift of swine
a stud of mares
a parliament of rooks & owls
a glozing of taverners
a covey of ptarmigan
a business of ferrets
a drunkship of cobblers
a sounder of wild boar
a nye of pheasants
a fall of woodcock
a sege of herons
a herd of curlews

US POSTAL SERVICE'S UNOFFICIAL MOTTO

*'Neither snow nor rain nor heat nor gloom of night stays these couriers
from the swift completion of their appointed rounds.'*

Inscription found on New York's General Post Office (8th & 33rd),
thought to originate from Herodotus' description of the Persian couriers
*c.*500BC, translated by Professor George H. Palmer of Harvard University.
Contrary to popular belief, the motto has no official link with the USPS.

THE FLAG OF GUADELOUPE

The flag consists of horizontal bands which, from the top down, are:
narrow green, thin white stripe, wide red band, thin white stripe, and
narrow green. A five-pointed gold star is located in the middle of the red
band, on the hoist side. The flag of France is flown for official occasions.

---SCOVILLE SCALE---

In 1912 Wilbur Scoville developed his now famous method to chart the comparative heat of different chillis (*J. Am. Pharm. Assoc.* 1912; 1:453–4). The greater number of Scoville Units, the hotter the chilli. For example:

Bell Pepper	0 *Scoville Units (SU)*
Peperocini, Cherry Pepper	100–500
New Mexico, Aji Panca	500–1,000
Ancho, Passila, Espanola	1,000–1,500
Sandia, Rocotillo, Cascabel, Poblano	1,500–2,500
Jalapeno, Mirasol	2,500–5,000
Chilcostle, Louisiana Hot	5,000–10,000
de Arbol, Serrano, Japones	10,000–30,000
Piquin, Aji, Cayenne, Tabasco	30,000–50,000
Chiltepin, Tepin	50,000–80,000
Habanero, Scotch Bonnet	80,000–300,000
Pure Capsaicin	16,000,000

This can only be a rough guide, since the heat of chillis can vary from pepper to pepper.

---HOW TO TIE A BOW TIE---

---A CERTAIN CHINESE ENCYCLOPEDIA---

Although possibly an elaborate literary joke, one of the most curious lists is that quoted (and perhaps invented) by J.L. Borges. In one of his essays (made famous by Michel Foucault), Borges claims that Dr Franz Kuhn discovered a 'certain Chinese encyclopedia' entitled *Celestial Empire of Benevolent Knowledge,* which stated that all animals can be classified thus:

[a] belonging to the Emperor · [b] embalmed · [c] tame
[d] sucking pigs · [e] sirens · [f] fabulous · [g] stray dogs
[h] included in the present classification · [i] that shake like a fool
[j] innumerable · [k] drawn with a very fine camel-hair brush
[l] etcetera · [m] having just broken the water pitcher
[n] that, if seen from a distance, look like flies.

---------------- THE ARAB LEAGUE ----------------

The Arab League, or the League of Arab States, was founded in Cairo in 1945 to 'promote economic, social, political, and military cooperation'.

Algeria · Bahrain · Comoros · Djibouti · Egypt · Iraq · Jordan
Kuwait · Lebanon · Libya · Mauritania · Morocco · Oman · Palestine
Qatar · Saudi Arabia · Somalia · Sudan · Syria · Tunisia
United Arab Emirates · Yemen

---------------- COUNTING FRUIT STONES ----------------

The following doggerels are traditional rhymes sung by generations of British schoolchildren. The rhymes tend to be associated with girls counting fruit stones left on their plates (each additional stone decreasing the value of their future husband, wedding dress, &c.). Perhaps most famously, John le Carré adapted one of the lines as a title for a spy novel.

When shall I marry? This year, next year, sometime, never.
What will my husband be?
Tinker, tailor, soldier, sailor, rich-man, poor-man, beggar-man, thief.
What shall I wear? Silk, satin, cotton, rags.
How shall I get it? Given, borrowed, bought, stolen.
How shall I get to church? Coach, carriage, wheelbarrow, cart.
Where shall I live? Big house, little house, pig-sty, barn.

---------------- THE AMERICAN CREED ----------------

'I believe in the United States of America as a government of the people, by the people, for the people; whose just powers are derived from the consent of the governed; a democracy in a republic; a sovereign Nation of many sovereign States; a perfect union, one and inseparable; established upon those principles of freedom, equality, justice, and humanity for which American patriots sacrificed their lives and fortunes. I therefore believe it is my duty to my country to love it, to support its Constitution, to obey its laws, to respect its flag, and to defend it against all enemies.'

The American Creed was written by William Tyler Page in 1917 as an entry for a national competition to find a composition which would embody the principles of America. The competition, conceived by Henry Sterling Chapin, the Commissioner of Education in New York, prompted over three thousand entries. Page's powerful text was formally adopted as the American Creed by the US House of Representatives in April 1918.

—— PRESIDENTS OF THE UNITED STATES ——

President	Inaug.	Party	Age took office	Left-handed	Born British	Owned slaves	Had facial hair	Bald / red hair	Mt. Rushmore	Assassinated	Served as V.P.	Unmarried	6'1" or taller	Quaker	At Harvard	Nobel Prize	State of birth	Served >1 term	Impeached	Died in office	Resigned	Died on 4th July	Born on 4th July	Sun sign	$ salary in office
George Washington	1789	Federalist	57		■	■		■	■				■				VA	■						♓	25,000
John Adams	1797	Federalist	61		■			■			■				■		MA					■		♏	25,000
Thomas Jefferson	1801	Dem.–Rep.	57		■	■		■	■		■		■				VA	■				■		♈	25,000
James Madison	1809	Dem.–Rep.	57		■	■											VA	■						♓	25,000
James Monroe	1817	Dem.–Rep.	58		■	■											VA	■				■		♉	25,000
John Q. Adams	1825	Dem.–Rep.	57		■										■		MA							♋	25,000
Andrew Jackson	1829	Democrat	61		■	■							■				SC	■						♓	25,000
Martin Van Buren	1837	Democrat	54			□	?	■									NY							♐	25,000
William Harrison	1841	Whig	68		■	■											VA			■				♒	25,000
John Tyler	1841	Whig	51			■					■						VA							♈	25,000
James Knox Polk	1845	Democrat	49			■											NC							♏	25,000
Zachary Taylor	1849	Whig	64			■											VA			■				♐	25,000
Millard Fillmore	1850	Whig	50								■						NY							♑	25,000
Franklin Pierce	1853	Democrat	48														NH							♐	25,000
James Buchanan	1857	Democrat	65									■					PA							♉	25,000
Abraham Lincoln	1861	Republican	52				■		■	■			■				KY	■		■				♒	25,000
Andrew Johnson	1865	Democrat	56			■					■						NC		■					♑	25,000
Ulysses S. Grant	1869	Republican	46			■	■										OH	■						♉	25 & 50
Rutherford Hayes	1877	Republican	54				■								■		OH							♎	50,000
James Garfield	1881	Republican	49	■			■			■							OH			■				♏	50,000
Chester Arthur	1881	Republican	51				■				■		■				VT							♎	50,000
Grover Cleveland	1885	Democrat	47				■										NJ							♓	50,000

PRESIDENTS OF THE UNITED STATES

President	Inauguration	Political party	Took office (age)	Birth state	$ salary paid in office
Benjamin Harrison	1889	Republican	55	OH	50,000
Grover Cleveland	1893	Democrat	54	NJ	50,000
William McKinley	1897	Republican	54	OH	50,000
Theodore Roosevelt	1901	Republican	42	NY	50,000
William Taft	1909	Republican	51	OH	75,000
Woodrow Wilson	1913	Democrat	56	VA	75,000
Warren Harding	1921	Republican	55	OH	75,000
Calvin Coolidge	1923	Republican	51	VT	75,000
Herbert Hoover	1929	Republican	54	IA	75,000
Franklin D. Roosevelt	1933	Democrat	51	NY	75,000
Harry S Truman	1945	Democrat	60	MO	75 & 100
Dwight Eisenhower	1953	Republican	62	TX	100,000
John F. Kennedy	1961	Democrat	43	MA	100,000
Lyndon B. Johnson	1963	Democrat	55	TX	100,000
Richard Nixon	1969	Republican	56	CA	200,000
Gerald Ford	1974	Republican	61	NE	200,000
James 'Jimmy' Carter	1977	Democrat	52	GA	200,000
Ronald Reagan	1981	Republican	69 ?	IL	200,000
George Bush	1989	Republican	64	MA	200,000
William 'Bill' Clinton	1993	Democrat	46	AR	200,000
George W. Bush	2001	Republican	54	CT	400,000

Many entries are the subject of debate & dispute, for example: Facial hair includes mutton-chop whiskers · A. Johnson's political allegiance is complex · Slave ownership not necessarily while President · Red-headedness is subjective (e.g. JFK) · Some Presidential heights are hard to confirm · etc. · Hollow boxes denote assassination attempt, or an obsolete banknote design.

---------------------------- BLOODY MARY ----------------------------

2 vodka · 3 tomato juice · ½ lemon juice · Ground salt & pepper
6 dashes Worcestershire sauce · 5 drops Tabasco · lemon & celery

–SOME UNCOMMON INTERNET DOMAIN CODES–

.ac . . Ascension Island	.im . . . . Isle of Man	.pn. . . . Pitcairn Island
.aw . . . . Aruba	.iq . . . . Iraq	.re. . . . Reunion Island
.bf. . . . . . Burkina Faso	.is . . . . Iceland	.sh . . . . St. Helena
.bj . . . . Benin	.ki. . . . . Kiribati	.sr . . . . Suriname
.bv. . . . . Bouvet Island	.kg. . . . . . . Kyrgyzstan	.tg . . . . Togo
.cx . . Christmas Island	.kz . . . . . . Kazakhstan	.tv . . . . Tuvalu
.er. . . . . Eritrea	.lv . . . . Latvia	.ug. . . . . Uganda
.fj. . . . . Fiji	.mc. . . . . Monaco	.va . . . . Holy See
.gg . . . . Guernsey	.mm . . . . . . Myanmar	.vu . . . . Vanuatu
.gp . . . . . . Guadeloupe	.no. . . . . Norway	.ye . . . . Yemen
.gw. . . . Guinea-Bissau	.nu. . . . . Niue	.yt. . . . . Mayotte
.ht . . . . Haiti	.om . . . . Oman	.za . . . . . . South Africa

------- BIKINI, DEFCON & HOMELAND SECURITY -------

The term BIKINI is employed by British armed forces around the world
to indicate the level of terrorist threat. The BIKINI ALERT STATES are:

WHITE · BLACK · BLACK SPECIAL · AMBER · RED

Each level indicates a greater degree of threat. BIKINI states are usually set
at a local level, indicating the perceived risk at specific locations. The US
Government operates a series of 'progressive alert postures' indicating the
overall level of combat readiness: DEFence CONditions. These are part of
a wider schemata of ALERTCONs and EMERGCONs. The DEFCON status
is from 5 (normal peacetime readiness) to 1 (maximum force readiness)
and while the DEFCON level is classified, some state that at the height of
the 1962 Cuban Missile Crisis, the US military advanced to DEFCON 2.
In March 2002 a new schemata of THREAT CONDITIONS was introduced by
the Department of Homeland Security to co-ordinate Federal, State, local,
and private response. From lowest to highest, the levels and their colors are:

LOW *green* · GUARDED *blue* · ELEVATED *yellow* · HIGH *orange* · SEVERE *red*

The Attorney General is responsible for assigning THREAT CONDITIONS,
which may be issued nationally, or to a specific location or industrial sector.

HOLALPHABETIC SENTENCES

Also known as Pangrams, these are sentences containing every letter of the alphabet, of particular interest to typographers when browsing fonts.

The quick brown fox jumps over the lazy dog
Waltz, bad nymph, for quick jigs vex
How piqued gymnasts can level six jumping razorback frogs
We promptly judged antique ivory buckles for the next prize
Sixty zippers were quickly picked from the woven jute bag
Jump by vow of quick, lazy strength in Oxford
Jackdaws love my big sphinx of quartz

THE FOUR CORNERS

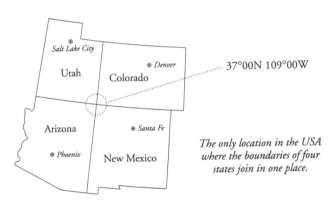

37°00N 109°00W

The only location in the USA where the boundaries of four states join in one place.

SOME NOTABLE CANADIANS

Pamela Anderson	*model*	Yousuf Karsh	*photographer*
Margaret Atwood	*author*	Marshall McLuhan	*media theorist*
Barenaked Ladies	*beat-combo*	James Naismith	*basketball inventor*
Conrad Black	*publisher*	Wilder Penfield	*neurosurgeon*
Jim Carrey	*comedian*	Oscar Peterson	*jazz pianist*
Leonard Cohen	*singer*	Paul Shaffer	*musician*
Douglas Coupland	*author*	Joe Shuster	*creator of Superman*
David Cronenberg	*director*	Donald Sutherland	*actor*
Celine Dion	*singer*	Cliff Thorburn	*snooker player*
J.K. Galbraith	*economist*	Gilles Villeneuve	*racing driver*
Erving Goffman	*micro-sociologist*	Neil Young	*musician*

——————— SOME NATIONAL ANTHEMS ———————

Brazil	*Ouviram Do Ipiranga Às Margens Plácidas*
China	*Yiyongjun Jinxingqu*
Cuba	*Al Combate, Corred Bayameses*
France	*La Marseillaise*
Grenada	*Hail Grenada, Land of Ours*
Haïti	*La Dessalinienne*
Iceland	*Lofsöngur*
Iran	*Sorûd-E Jomhûri-Ye Eslâmi*
Israel	*Hatikvah*
Kiribati	*Teirake Kain Kiribati*
Mexico	*Mexicanos, Al Grito De Guerra*
Federated States of Micronesia	*Patriots of Micronesia*
Nauru	*Nauru Bwiema*
Nigeria	*Arise, O Compatriots*
Russia	*Russia, Sacred Our Empire*
St. Kitts and Nevis	*Oh Land of Beauty*
Singapore	*Majullah Singapura*
Vietnam	*Tien Quan Ca*

———LINES OF THE LONDON UNDERGROUND———

Line	Length	Opened c.	Busiest Station	Color	Stations
Bakerloo	23.2 *km*	1906	Oxford Circus	brown	25
Central	74	1900	Oxford Circus	red	49
Circle	22.5	1863–5	Victoria	yellow	27
District	64	1868	Victoria	green	60
East London	8	1843–63	Canada Water	orange	9
Hammersmith	26.5	1863–4	King's Cross	pink	28
Jubilee[†]	36.2	1880[‡]	Bond Street	silver	27
Metropolitan	66.7	1868	Baker Street	maroon	34
Northern	58	1890	Leicester Square	black	51
Piccadilly	71	1906	Piccadilly Circus	navy blue	52
Victoria	21	1968	Victoria	light blue	16
Waterloo & City	2.4	1898	—	cyan	2

[†] *The only line which interconnects with every other line.* [‡] *Inaugurated 1979.*

———THE FIVE REGULAR PLATONIC SOLIDS———

Regular polyhedron	Faces		
tetrahedron	4 triangles	octahedron	8 triangles
cube	6 squares	dodecahedron	12 pentagons
		icosahedron	20 triangles

THE BOND FILMS

FILM TITLE	007	YEAR	VILLAIN	BOND GIRL	KEY CAR
Dr No	SC	62	Doctor No	Ursula Andress · Honey Ryder	Sunbeam Alpine
From Russia With Love	SC	63	Red Grant	Daniela Bianchi · Tatiana Romanova	Bentley Mark IV
Goldfinger	SC	64	Goldfinger	Honor Blackman · Pussy Galore	Aston Martin DB5
Thunderball	SC	65	Emilio Largo	Claudine Auger · Domino	Aston Martin DB5
You Only Live Twice	SC	67	Blofeld	Akiko Wakabayashi · Aki	Toyota 2000 GT
On Her Majesty's Secret Service	GL	69	Blofeld	Diana Rigg · Tracy Vicenzo	Aston Martin DBS
Diamonds Are Forever	SC	71	Blofeld	Jill St John · Tiffany Case	Moon Buggy
Live And Let Die	RM	73	Dr Kananga	Jane Seymour · Solitaire	Double Decker
The Man With The Golden Gun	RM	74	Scaramanga	Britt Ekland · Mary Goodnight	AMC Hornet
The Spy Who Loved Me	RM	77	Karl Stromberg	Barbara Bach · Anya Amasova	Lotus Esprit
Moonraker	RM	79	Hugo Drax	Lois Chiles · Dr Holly Goodhead	Gondola
For Your Eyes Only	RM	81	Kristatos	Carole Bouquet · Melina Havelock	Citroën 2CV
Octopussy	RM	83	Kamal Khan	Maud Adams · Octopussy	Mercedes 250SE
A View To A Kill	RM	85	Max Zorin	Tanya Roberts · Stacey Sutton	Renault 11
The Living Daylights	TD	87	Koskov	Maryam D'Abo · Kara Milovy	Aston Martin Volante
Licence To Kill	TD	89	Franz Sanchez	Carey Lowell · Pam Bouvier	Kentworth Tanker
GoldenEye	PB	95	Alec Trevelyan	Izabell Scorupco · Natalya Simonova	BMW Z3
Tomorrow Never Dies	PB	97	Elliott Carver	Michelle Yeoh · Wai Lin	BMW 750iL
The World Is Not Enough	PB	99	Renard	Denise Richards · Christmas Jones	BMW Z8
Die Another Day	PB	02	Zao	Halle Berry · Jinx	Aston Martin V12 Vanquish

[007s: SC – Sean Connery · GL – George Lazenby · RM – Roger Moore · TD – Timothy Dalton · PB – Pierce Brosnan]

COCKNEY RHYMING SLANG

Cockney refers to the working-class of London's East End, traditionally those born within earshot of the bells of St Mary-le-Bow Church in Cheapside. Cockney rhyming slang replaces the intended word with a rhyming couplet – only the first word of which is usually spoken. For example, the word 'phone' would be replaced by the phrase 'dog and bone', but in conversation only the word 'dog' would be said. This has the advantage of confusing the uninitiated, making cockney rhyming slang ideal for those, like street traders, who wish to communicate in private.

Adam and Eve............Believe	Gregory Peck..............Check
Alan Whickers...........Knickers	Hampton Wick.............Prick
Apples and Pears............Stairs	Hank Marvin............Starving
Aristotle (Harris)..........Bottle	Jam Jar........................Car
Artful Dodger.............Lodger	Jimmy Riddle.............Piddle
Ascot Races.................Braces	Aunt Joanna................Piano
Ball and Chalk..............Walk	Khyber Pass.....................Ass
Barnaby Rudge.............Judge	Kick and Prance...........Dance
Barnet Fair...................Hair	Lady Godiva.................Fiver
Battlecruiser..............Boozer	Lionel Blairs................Flares
Boat Race....................Face	Loaf of Bread...............Head
Bob Hope...................Soap	Mickey Bliss..................Piss
Boracic Lint.................Skint	Mince Pies....................Eyes
Brahms and Liszt...........Pissed	Mork and Mindy.........Windy
Brass Tacks..................Facts	Mutt and Jeff................Deaf
Bread and Honey..........Money	North and South.........Mouth
Bricks and Mortar......Daughter	Oily Rag........................Fag
Bristol City..................Titty	Peckham Rye..................Tie
Brown Bread.................Dead	Pen and Ink.................Stink
Butcher's Hook..............Look	Plates of Meat................Feet
Chalfont St Giles............Piles	Pony and Trap...............Crap
Chalk Farm...................Arm	Porky Pies......................Lies
China Plate...................Mate	Richard the 3rd.............Turd
Cobbler's Awls...............Balls	Rosie Lee.......................Tea
Cock and Hen.................Ten	Rub-a-Dub.....................Pub
Currant Bun....................Sun	Skin and Blister.............Sister
Daisy Roots.................Boots	Sky Rocket................Pocket
Darby and Joan.............Moan	Sweeney Todd.......Flying Squad
Dicky Bird....................Word	Syrup of Figs.................Wig
Dicky Dirt....................Shirt	Tea Leaf.......................Thief
Dog and Bone.............Phone	Tit for Tat ('Titfer')...........Hat
Duke of Kent.................Rent	Tom-foolery............Jewellery
Dustbin Lid.....................Kid	Trouble and Strife..........Wife
Frog and Toad...............Road	Whistle and Flute............Suit

ORDERS TO FIRE CANNON

Firing a single shot from a stowed and loaded cannon in Nelson's navy was regulated by the following sequence of orders:

Silence!
Cast loose your gun!
Level your gun!
Take out your tampion!
Prime!
Run out your gun!
Point your gun!
Fire!
Worm and sponge!
Load with cartridge!
Load with shot and wad to your shot!
Ram home shot and wad!
Put in your tampion!
House your gun!
Secure your gun!

COMMONPLACE SPANISH

A caballo	on horseback
Aficionado	an (often amateur) enthusiast
Amigo	friend
A vuestra salud!	cheers!
Barba a barba	face to face [beard to beard]
Caballero	a horseman; a gentleman or knight
Capa y espada	cloak and dagger, intrigue
Contrabandista	smuggler
En casa	at home
Gringo	foreigner (often pejorative)
Hacienda	grand estate or plantation
Hasta la vista	see you later
Hasta mañana	see you tomorrow
Junta	a military group, often with political power
Lo pasado, pasado	'what is past is past'
Mayordomo	the head servant or steward [major-domo]
Peccadillo	minor transgression; personal (sexual) habit
Que sera sera	'what will be will be'
Salud y pesetas	'health and fortune'
Siglo de oro	a golden age; in Spain, that of 16thC & early 17thC
Vigilante	self appointed (unofficial) arbiter of justice

DR JOHNSON

One of the towering literary figures of his age, Samuel Johnson (1709–84) was a lexicographer, dramatist, novelist, critic, poet, editor, and conversationalist. Johnson's verbal dexterity (immortalized in great part by his companion and biographer James Boswell) demonstrates a masterful command of English, and shows his unique insight into human nature.

WORK & MONEY

No man but a blockhead ever wrote, except for money.

Faults and defects every work of man must have.

Whatever you have, spend less.

What we hope ever to do with ease, we must learn first to do with diligence.

As peace is the end of war, so to be idle is the ultimate purpose of the busy.

Those who attain to any excellence commonly spend life in some single pursuit, for excellence is not often gained upon easier terms.

It is wonderful when a calculation is made, how little the mind is actually employed in the discharge of any profession.

All intellectual improvement arises from leisure.

The true art of memory is the art of attention.

LANGUAGE

In all pointed sentences, some degree of accuracy must be sacrificed to conciseness.

Example is always more efficacious than precept.

Read over your compositions, and where ever you meet with a passage which you think is particularly fine, strike it out.

Every quotation contributes something to the stability or enlargement of the language.

Dictionaries are like watches, the worst is better than none, and the best cannot be expected to go quite true.

The end of writing is to instruct; the end of poetry is to instruct by pleasing.

FOOD & DRINK

Claret is the liquor for boys; port for men; but he who aspires to be a hero ... must drink brandy.

A cucumber should be well sliced, and dressed with pepper and vinegar, and then thrown out, as good for nothing.

SHAKESPEARE

[Shakespeare] sacrifices virtue to convenience, and is so much more careful to please than to instruct, that he seems to write without any moral purpose.

DR JOHNSON cont.

FRIENDSHIP

If a man does not make new acquaintance as he advances through life, he will soon find himself alone. A man should keep his friendship in constant repair.

Always, Sir, set a high value on spontaneous kindness.

To let friendship die away by negligence and silence is certainly not wise. It is voluntarily to throw away one of the greatest comforts of the weary pilgrimage.

Distance has the same effect on the mind as on the eye.

The longer we live the more we think and the higher the value we put on friendship and tenderness towards parents and friends.

How few of his friends' houses would a man choose to be at when he is ill.

HUMAN NATURE

Almost every man wastes part of his life attempting to display qualities which he doesn't possess.

Nothing can please many, and please long, but just representations of general nature.

Nothing is more hopeless than a scheme of merriment.

Whoever thinks of going to bed before twelve o'clock is a scoundrel.

It is wonderful that five thousand years have now elapsed since the creation of the world, and still it is undecided whether or not there has ever been an instance of the spirit of any person appearing after death. All argument is against it; but all belief is for it.

All envy would be extinguished, if it were universally known that there are none to be envied.

We are all prompted by the same motives, all deceived by the same fallacies, all animated by hope, obstructed by danger, entangled by desire, and seduced by pleasure.

It matters not how a man dies, but how he lives. The act of dying is not of importance, it lasts so short a time.

He was dull in a new way, and that made many people think him great.

LONDON

Sir, if you wish to have a just notion of the magnitude of this city, you must not be satisfied with seeing its great streets and squares, but must survey the innumerable little lanes and courts. It is not in the showy evolutions of buildings, but in the multiplicity of human habitations which are crowded together, that the wonderful immensity of London consists.

When a man is tired of London, he is tired of life; for there is in London all that life can afford.

── CONSTITUTIONAL AMENDMENTS (IN BRIEF) ──

1st .... Freedom of religion, speech, press, assembly, and petition
2nd .... The right to keep and bear arms
3rd .... Prevention of compulsory billetting during peacetime
4th .... Security of person and possessions against search and seizure
5th ...... Prevention of double-jeopardy; right against self-incrimination
6th .... Fair, speedy, and public trial by jury; right to counsel
7th .... Right to trial by jury in common law suits
8th ..... Prevention of cruel or unusual punishments; and excessive fines
9th .... Protection of rights not enumerated in the Constitution
10th .... Reservation of the rights of individual States
11th .... Delineation of judicial powers of the US in certain cases
12th .... Procedures for electing President & Vice President
13th .... Abolished slavery
14th .... Guarantee of the rights of citizenship
15th .... Right to vote regardless of race, color, or previous servitude
16th .... Right of Congress to levy income taxes
17th .... Procedure for electing Senators
18th .... Introduced prohibition
19th .... Right of women to vote
20th .... Presidential term and succession; terms of other offices
21st .... Repeal of prohibition (18th Amendment)
22nd .... Limiting Presidents to two terms
23rd ... Grants Washington DC residents a vote in Presidential elections
24th .... Bars poll (voting) tax in federal elections
25th .... Order of Presidential succession
26th .... Right to vote at age eighteen
27th .... Postpones Representatives' pay rises until after new elections

────────── HOLLYWOOD WALK OF FAME ──────────

The location of some of the double acts who are on the Hollywood Walk of Fame which runs down Hollywood Boulevard (HB) & Vine Street (VS).

1611 VS .... Budd Abbott & Lou Costello .... 6438 HB
6756 HB .... Fred Astaire & Ginger Rogers........... 6772 HB
7021 HB................ Stan Laurel & Oliver Hardy .... 1500 VS
6322 HB......... Humphrey Bogart & Lauren Bacall............ 1724 VS
6817 HB .... Tony Curtis & Jack Lemmon .... 6357 HB
7018 HB .... Sonny & Cher..................... 7018 HB
6541 HB................. Bob Hope & Bing Crosby .... 1611 VS
6357 HB .... Jack Lemmon & Walter Matthau .... 6357 HB
6901 HB.............. John Travolta & Olivia Newton-John .... 6925 HB

THE US FLAG

The correct proportions of the US Flag (the Stars & Stripes) were laid down on August 21 1959 by Executive Order of President Eisenhower:

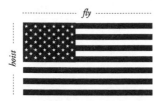

If *hoist* = 1, other proportions are:

fly	1.9
union hoist	0.5385
union fly	0.76
width of stripe	0.0769
diameter of star	0.0616

The US Code lays down rules relating to the flag, some of which are:

It is the universal custom to display the flag only from sunrise to sunset on buildings and on stationary flagstaffs in the open. However, when a patriotic effect is desired, the flag may be displayed 24 hours a day if properly illuminated during the hours of darkness · the flag should be hoisted briskly and lowered ceremoniously · the flag should not be displayed on days when the weather is inclement, except when an all-weather flag is displayed · the flag should be displayed in or near every polling place on election day · the flag should never touch anything beneath it, such as the ground, the floor, water, or merchandise · the flag should never be used as a covering for a ceiling · the flag should never be used as a receptacle for receiving, holding, carrying, or delivering anything · the flag should never be used for advertising purposes in any manner whatsoever · no part of the flag should ever be used as a costume or athletic uniform · the flag, when it is in such condition that it is no longer a fitting emblem for display, should be destroyed in a dignified way, preferably by burning.

The history and design of the US Flag are steeped in myth and dispute. One of the earliest facts commonly agreed is the resolution passed by the Marine Committee of the 2nd Continental Congress at Philadelphia (June 14, 1777) which reads: *'That the flag of the United States be thirteen stripes, alternate red and white; that the union be thirteen stars, white in a blue field, representing a new constellation.'* The 1777 flag was used until 1795 when two more stars and stripes were added to recognise the admission of Vermont and Kentucky. To avoid cluttering the flag with stripes, Congress decreed (1818) that the flag should have 13 stripes, and that new admissions to the Union should be recognised with a new star. The 50-star flag was raised for the first time at 12:01 a.m. on July 4 1960, at Fort McHenry National Monument, when Hawaii joined the Union.

MURDERS

term	*killing of a*		
homicide	person	sororicide	sister
genocide	ethnic /national group	mariticide	spouse
suicide	self	infanticide	infant
parenticide	parent	uxoricide	wife
patricide	father	parricide	kinsman
matricide	mother	regicide	king
fratricide	brother	tyrannicide	tyrant
		vaticide	prophet

CLASSICAL COLUMN TYPES

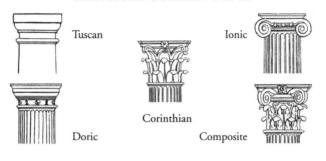

Tuscan

Ionic

Corinthian

Doric

Composite

MARTINI

⅓ Vermouth · ⅔ Dry Gin · *Garnish, serve on or off the rocks.*
(Although James Bond always shaked, to avoid dilution, one should stir.)

COUNTRIES WITH COMPULSORY VOTING

Argentina · Australia · Austria · Belgium · Bolivia · Brazil · Chile
Congo · Costa Rica · Cyprus · Dominican Rep. · Ecuador · Egypt
El Salvador · Fiji · Greece · Honduras · Lebanon · Libya · Liechtenstein
Luxembourg · Madagascar · Mexico · Nauru · Panama · Paraguay
Philippines · Singapore · Thailand · Turkey · Uruguay · Venezuela

---

CAVIAR

Caviar derives from the Turkish term for fish-eggs: *khavia*. Traditionally,
3 sturgeon species are fished for caviar: BELUGA, OSIETRA, & SEVRUGA.

———————— SOME FAMOUS HORSES ————————

LAMRI . . . . King Arthur	KANTAKA . . . . Buddha
BLACKIE . . . . Chief Sitting Bull	FUBUKI . . . . Emperor Hirohito
MAGNOLIA . . . George Washington	SILVER . . . . The Lone Ranger
STRYMON . . . . Xerxes	HAIZUM . . . . Archangel Gabriel
BLACK BESS . . . . Dick Turpin	COPENHAGEN . . . . Wellington
ROSINANTE . . . . Don Quixote	SHADOWFAX . . . . Gandalf
ARION . . . . Hercules	BUCEPHALUS . . Alexander the Great
MARENGO[†] . . . . Napoleon	TRIGGER . . . . Roy Rogers
HIPPOCAMPUS . . . . Neptune	PHALLUS . . . . Heraclius
VIC . . . . Lt.-Col. Custer	SAVOY . . . . Charles VIII

[†]*Marengo was captured by the British. He outlived Napoleon by eight years, and his skeleton is preserved at London's National Army Museum. A snuff-box was made from one of his hoofs.*

———————— BLOOD GROUP COMPATIBILITY ————————

Group may receive:	Plasma from	Whole Blood from	Red Cells from
O+	any O; A, B or AB	O+, O-	O+, O-
O-	any O; A B or AB	O-	O-
A+	any A or AB	any A+, A-	any A+; A-; O+, O-
A-	any A or AB	A-	any A- or O-
B+	any B or AB	any B+ or B-	any B+; B-; O+ or O-
B-	any B or AB	B-	any B- or O-
AB+	any AB	any AB+ or AB-	any AB+; AB- A+, A-, B+, B-, O+, O-
AB-	AB	AB-	any AB-; A- B-, or O-

The above table must not be used as a guide, since many anomalies exist and un-crossmatched transfusions can cause life-threatening reactions.

UNTIMELY DEATHS OF MUSICIANS

POP STAR	murder	drugs 'n' alcohol	suicide	plane crash	traffic accident	misadventure	CAUSE OF DEATH	AGED
Chet Baker						■	*death by defenestration*	58
Marc Bolan					■		*overdose of tree while driving*	29
John Bonham		■					*Led Zeppelin; vodka overdose*	32
Sonny Bono						■	*skied into a tree in Tahoe*	62
Jeff Buckley						■	*drowned in Mississippi River*	30
Tim Buckley		■					*mistook heroin for cocaine*	28
Karen Carpenter			■				*rock'n'roll underdose: anorexia*	32
Steve Clark		■					*Def Leppard; drink and drugs*	30
Kurt Cobain			■				*Nirvana; suicide (or murder?)*	27
Eddie Cochran					■		*car crash on his way to airport*	21
Sam Cooke	■						*shot dead by a motel owner*	33
King Curtis	■						*murdered outside his own home*	37
'Mama' Cass						■	*ham sandwich asphyxiation?*	32
Jerry Garcia		■					*Gratefully Dead via heroin*	53
Marvin Gaye	■						*shot dead by his father*	44
Lowell George		■					*Little Feat; big drug overdose*	34
Jimi Hendrix		■					*Drug overdose (suicide?)*	27
Buddy Holly				■			*killed in 'that' plane crash*	22
M. Hutchence			■				*suicide in his hotel room*	37
Brian Jones						■	*drowned in his swimming pool*	27
Janis Joplin		■					*accidental heroin overdose*	27
Paul Kossoff		■					*drug-induced heart attack*	25
John Lennon	■						*murdered by Mark Chapman*	40
Kirsty MacColl						■	*tragic jet-ski collision*	41
Joe Meek			■				*shot his landlady, and himself*	37
Keith Moon						■	*drink, drugs, and general excess*	31
Jim Morrison		■					*drink and possibly heroin too*	27
'Notorious' B.I.G.	■						*capped in a gangster-rap war*	24
Elvis Presley		■					*prescription drug-abuse*	42
Otis Redding				■			*killed in plane crash*	26
J.P. Richardson				■			*killed in 'that' plane crash*	28
Tupac Shakur	■						*capped in a gangster-rap war*	25
Vivian Stanshall						■	*Bonzo Dog Band; died in fire*	51
Ritchie Valens				■			*killed in 'that' plane crash*	17
Stevie Ray Vaughan				■			*helicopter flew into mountain*	35
Sid Vicious		■					*Sex Pistols; heroin overdose*	21
Gene Vincent		■					*general rock'n'roll excess*	36
Dennis Wilson						■	*drowned: Beach Boy not Buoy*	39

SUPER BOWL SINGERS

The first Super Bowl in 1967 saw Green Bay beat Kansas City 35 to 10. Below, those who have sung the National Anthem at the Super Bowl:

SuperBowl	Performer
37	Dixie Chicks
36	Mariah Carey
35	Backstreet Boys
34	Faith Hill
33	Cher
32	Jewel
31	Luther Vandross
30	Vanessa Williams
29	Kathie Lee Gifford
28	Natalie Cole
27	Garth Brooks
26	Harry Connick Jr.
25	Whitney Houston
24	Aaron Neville
23	Billy Joel
22	Herb Alpert
21	Neil Diamond
20	Wynton Marsalis
19	San Francisco Children's Choir
18	Barry Manilow
17	Leslie Esterbrook
16	Diana Ross
15	Helen O'Connell
14	Cheryl Ladd
13	The Colgate Thirteen
12	Phyllis Kelly
11	Vicki Carr
10	Tom Sullivan
9	Grambling University Band
8	Charley Pride
7	Holy Angels Church
6	USAF Academy Chorale
5	Tommy Loy
4	Al Hirt
3	Anita Bryant
2	Grambling University Band
1	Arizona & Michigan Unis.

NATO ALPHABET

letter	code
A	Alpha
B	Bravo
C	Charlie
D	Delta
E	Echo
F	Foxtrot
G	Golf
H	Hotel
I	India
J	Juliet
K	Kilo
L	Lima
M	Mike
N	November
O	Oscar
P	Papa
Q	Quebec
R	Romeo
S	Sierra
T	Tango
U	Uniform
V	Victor
W	Whisky
X	X-ray
Y	Yankee
Z	Zulu

'AVERAGES'

With the following list of values: 10, 10, 20, 30, 30, 30, 40, 50, 70, 100

MEAN	the sum divided by the number of values	39
MODE	the most popular value	30
MEDIAN	the 'middle' value, here: (30+30) / 2	30
RANGE	the difference between the highest & lowest value	90

BALLISTIC MISSILE RANGES

SRBM	Short Range Ballistic Missile	<1,000 km
MRBM	Medium Range Ballistic Missile	1,000–3,000 km
IRBM	Intermediate Range Ballistic Missile	3,000–5,500 km
ICBM	Intercontinental Ballistic Missile	>5,500 km

POLARI

Polari is the theatrical and homosexual slang prevalent in London during the 1950s and '60s. An eclectic mix of Italian, Romany, back-slang, Yiddish, naval slang, and theatre-speak, Polari first entered the public domain through BBC radio's *Round The Horne*. Here, Kenneth Williams and Hugh Paddick, playing the theatrical Julian and Sandy, 'scandalized' and delighted the British public every week with louche, camp innuendo.

balonie	rubbish
bijou	small
blag	pick up
bona	good
bona nochi	good night
buvare	a drink
cackle	talk, gossip
charper	to search
clobber	clothes
dinarly	money
dish	ass
dolly	pleasant
dona	woman
drag	clothes
eek	face
fantabulosa	excellent
lallies	legs
lattie	house
lilly (law)	police
mangarie	food
mince	walk (effeminately)
nanty	not, no, none
naff	dull; straight
ogle	look, admire
omi	man
omi-palone	homosexual
palone	woman
riah	hair
scarper	to run off
shush bag	hold-all
slap	makeup
todd (Sloane)	alone
trolling	to mince, walk
vada	see, look at
vogue	cigarette
yews	eyes

'vada that bona omi with his dolly eek and fantabulosa riah'

THIRTY DAYS

Thirty days hath September, April, June, and November;
All the rest have thirty-one, Excepting February alone,
Which hath but twenty-eight days clear,
And twenty-nine in each leap year.

———— SOME PALMISTRY LINES ————

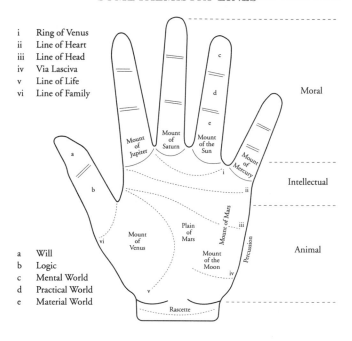

i   Ring of Venus
ii   Line of Heart
iii   Line of Head
iv   Via Lasciva
v   Line of Life
vi   Line of Family

Moral

Intellectual

Animal

a   Will
b   Logic
c   Mental World
d   Practical World
e   Material World

———— LAWS OF ROBOTICS ————

Although hinted at in some of his earlier works, Isaac Asimov's famous 3 Laws of Robotics were first explicitly stated in his 1942 story *Runaround.*

FIRST	SECOND	THIRD	ZEROTH
A robot may not injure a human being or, through inaction, allow a human being to come to harm.	*A robot must obey orders given it by human beings except where such orders would conflict with the 1st Law.*	*A robot must protect its own existence as long as such protection does not conflict with the 1st or 2nd Law.*	*A robot may not injure humanity or, through inaction, allow humanity to come to harm.*

Asimov later felt that his initial three laws were insufficient to protect society at large. Consequently, in his 1985 book *Robots and Empire,* he created a prequel, 'Zeroth' law, to which the other laws were subordinate.

THE DEMON'S DICTIONARY

Ambrose Bierce (1842–*c.*1914), was a remarkable man: a veteran of the American Civil War, a writer, poet, journalist, and – most memorably – the creator of *The Demon's Dictionary* (aka *The Devil's Dictionary*). The caustic and cynical definitions of 'The American Swift' survive the test of time, and still speak to his intended audience: 'enlightened souls who prefer dry wines to sweet, sense to sentiment, wit to humour, and clean English to slang'. Shown below are some of the more pungent entries:

ACHIEVEMENT · The death of endeavour and the birth of disgust.

ACTUALLY · Perhaps; possibly.

ADORE · To venerate expectantly.

ARMOR · The kind of clothing worn by a man whose tailor is a blacksmith.

AUCTIONEER · A man who proclaims with a hammer that he has picked a pocket with his tongue.

BAROMETER · An ingenious instrument which indicates what kind of weather we are having.

BORE · A person who talks when you wish him to listen.

COURT FOOL · The plaintiff.

COWARD · One who in a perilous emergency thinks with his legs.

DENTIST · A prestidigitator who, putting metal into your mouth, pulls coins out of your pocket.

ENVELOPE · The coffin of a document; the scabbard of a bill; the husk of a remittance; the bedgown of a love-letter.

ERUDITION · Dust shaken out of a book into an empty skull.

FAMOUS · Conspicuously miserable.

FIDELITY · A virtue peculiar to those who are about to be betrayed.

FOREFINGER · The finger commonly used in pointing out two malefactors.

FROG · A reptile with edible legs.

GHOST · The outward and visible sign of an inward fear.

HABIT · A shackle for the free.

HERMIT · A person whose vices and follies are not sociable.

HOPE · Desire and expectation rolled into one.

HOSPITALITY · The virtue which induces us to feed and lodge certain persons who are not in need of food and lodging.

ILLUSTRIOUS · Suitably placed for the shafts of malice, envy and detraction.

IMPIETY · Your irreverence toward my deity.

INFLUENCE · In politics, a visionary *quo* given in exchange for a substantial *quid*.

INSURRECTION · An unsuccessful revolution. Disaffection's failure to substitute misrule for bad government.

KILT · A costume sometimes worn by Scotchmen in America and Americans in Scotland.

LANGUAGE · The music with which we charm the serpents guarding another's treasure.

LITIGATION · A machine which you go into as a pig and come out of as a sausage.

MAUSOLEUM · The final and funniest folly of the rich.

MISFORTUNE · The kind of fortune that never misses.

PAINTING · The art of protecting flat surfaces from the weather and exposing them to the critic.

POLITICS · The conduct of public affairs for private advantage.

PRAY · To ask that the laws of the universe be annulled in behalf of a single petitioner confessedly unworthy.

PRICE · Value, plus a reasonable sum for the wear and tear of conscience in demanding it.

RIOT · A popular entertainment given to the military by innocent bystanders.

SATIETY · The feeling that one has for the plate after he has eaten its contents.

SELF-EVIDENT · Evident to one's self and to nobody else.

TELEPHONE · An invention of the devil which abrogates some of the advantages of making a disagreeable person keep his distance.

TWICE · Once too often.

ZEAL · A certain nervous disorder afflicting the young and inexperienced.

———————— SOME CHEMICAL ABBREVIATIONS ————————

TCP	Trichlorophenylmethyliodosalicyl	*germicide*
TNT	2,4,6-Trinitromethylbenzene	*explosive*
PCP	Phencyclidine	*hallucinogen*
LSD	Lysergic acid diethylamide	*hallucinogen*
DDT	Dichlorodiphenyltrichloroethane	*insecticide*
GTN	Glyceryl Trinitrate	*cardiac medication*

SOME MEDICAL SHORTHAND

A&O............alert and oriented	MS..............multiple sclerosis
AAA...abdominal aortic aneurysm	MVA.......motor vehicle accident
ac.....................before food	N(&)V.......nausea and vomiting
AS..................aortic stenosis	od......................once daily
bid.....................twice daily	PMH........past medical history
BP..................blood pressure	PN................percussion note
CBC........complete blood count	PND.......paroxysmal nocturnal
CHOL..................cholesterol	dyspnea (waking SOB)
CP......................chest pain	PR.....................per rectum
CT.....computerized tomography	prn.................when required
CVA......cerebrovascular accident	PSA......prostate specific antigen
CXR....................chest X-ray	PUD..........peptic ulcer disease
D&C.....dilatation and curettage	qid...............four times a day
DTP.diphtheria, tetanus, pertussis	RBC..............red blood count
DVT........deep vein thrombosis	ROS.............review of systems
Dx......................diagnosis	Rx........treatment, prescription
EPIG....................epigastric	sc.................sub-cutaneous
FH..................family history	SH...................social history
H&H..............hemoglobin &	sl......................sub-lingual
hematocrit	SOB..........shortness of breath
HGB.................hemoglobin	TB.....................tuberculosis
Hct....................hematocrit	TIA......transient ischemic attack
HT.........................height	tid...............three times a day
IMP....................impression	T&A............tonsillectomy and
IUP........intrauterine pregnancy	adenoidectomy
LFT's...........liver function tests	TRIG..................triglycerides
LMP.........last menstrual period	UA...................urine analysis
loc...........loss of consciousness	US.....................ultrasound
M&M....morbidity and mortality	WBC..........white blood count
MCV...mean corpuscular volume	WNWD...........well nourished,
MI..........myocardial infarction	well developed
MMR....measles, mumps, rubella	WGT.......................weight
MRI..magnetic resonance imaging	y/o........................year old

MISS AMERICA HAIR COLOR

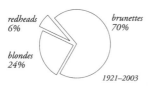

redheads 6%
brunettes 70%
blondes 24%
1921–2003

The Miss America title has been awarded (with some breaks) since 1921, when it was presented to Margaret Gorman. The statistics of winners' hair color might disprove the oft quoted claim that 'gentlemen prefer blondes'.

—————————— THE STATUE OF LIBERTY ——————————

Ground to tip of torch ..... 305'1"	Distance across the eye........ 2'6"
Heel to top of head .... 111'1"	Length of nose................ 4'6"
Length of hand .... 16'5"	Length of right arm .... 42'0"
Index finger.................. 8'0"	Thickness of right arm ...... 12'0"
Chin to cranium............. 17'3"	Thickness of waist........... 35'0"
Ear to ear.................... 10'0"	Total statue weight....... 225 tons
Width of mouth.............. 3'0"	Steps to the Crown........... 354

...Give me your tired, your poor; your huddled masses
yearning to breathe free, The wretched refuse of your
teeming shore, Send these, the homeless, tempest-tost,
to me: I lift my lamp beside the golden door.

From the pedestal inscription by Emma Lazarus, 1883

—————————————— HORSEPOWER ——————————————

Devised by James Watt (1736–1819), Horsepower is the power required to lift 550 pounds by 1 foot in 1 second: 33,000 foot-pounds per minute. 1 Horsepower = 745.7 watts; or 2,545 BTUs (British Thermal Units) per hour.

————————————— SOCCER WORLD CUP —————————————

YEAR	HOST	MASCOT	FINAL LINE UP	SCORE
1930	Uruguay	N/A	Uruguay *beat* Argentina	4-2
1934	Italy	N/A	Italy *beat* Czechoslovakia	2-1
1938	France	N/A	Italy *beat* Hungary	4-2
1950	Brazil	N/A	Uruguay *beat* Brazil	2-1
1954	Switzerland	N/A	W. Germany *beat* Hungary	3-2
1958	Sweden	N/A	Brazil *beat* Sweden	5-2
1962	Chile	N/A	Brazil *beat* Czechoslovakia	3-1
1966	England	Willie	England *beat* W. Germany	4-2
1970	Mexico	Juanito	Brazil *beat* Italy	4-1
1974	W. Germany	Tip & Tap	W. Germany *beat* Holland	2-1
1978	Argentina	Gauchito	Argentina *beat* Holland	3-1
1982	Spain	Naranjito	Italy *beat* W. Germany	3-1
1986	Mexico	Pique	Argentina *beat* W. Germany	3-2
1990	Italy	Ciao	Germany *beat* Argentina	1-0
1994	USA	Striker	Brazil *beat* Italy [on penalties]	3-2
1998	France	Footix	France *beat* Brazil	3-0
2002	Japan/S.Korea	Kaz, Ato, Nik	Brazil *beat* Germany	2-0

THE BRITISH RIOT ACT

'Our Sovereign Lord the King chargeth and commandeth all persons, being assembled, immediately to disperse themselves, and peaceably to depart to their habitations, or to their lawful business, upon the pains contained in the Act made in the first year of King George the First for preventing tumults and riotous assemblies. God Save the King.'

Under the Riot Act 1714, once a magistrate had read this passage within the hearing of a crowd greater than twelve, the 'rioters' had one hour to disperse before their presence ceased to be a misdemeanor and became a felony, ultimately punishable by death. The wording had to be read exactly as written, since at least one conviction was overturned because *'God Save the King'* had been left out. The Riot Act was repealed in 1973.

PROVERBIALLY, YOU CAN'T

... have it both ways
... have your cake and eat it[†]
... get blood out of a stone
... make an omelette without breaking eggs
... make a silk purse out of a sow's ear
... run with the hare and hunt with the hounds
... teach an old dog new tricks
... judge a book by its cover
... shake hands with a clenched fist
... tell which way the train went, by looking at the track
... win arguments by interrupting speakers
... have a rainbow without rain
... pick up two melons with one hand
... fool all of the people all of the time
... sip soup with a knife
... see the sky through a bamboo tube
... measure the sea with a shell
... cheat an honest man
... catch a cub without going into the tiger's den

[†]There is a school of thought that maintains 'you can't eat your cake and have it' is a more logical construction.

NATO COUNTRIES

Belgium · Canada · Czech Rep. · Denmark · France · Germany · Greece
Hungary · Iceland · Italy · Luxembourg · Netherlands · Norway
Poland · Portugal · Spain · Turkey · United Kingdom · United States

—— TIME MAGAZINE'S PERSON OF THE YEAR ——

Each year since 1927, TIME Magazine has announced its 'Person of the Year' to the individual, cohort, idea, or object that has had the greatest influence on events of the preceding year – for good or ill. The following is a selection from this astonishing roll-call of significant historical figures.

'27 . . . . Charles Lindbergh	'72 . . . . Nixon & Kissinger
'30 . . . . Mohandas Gandhi	'74 . . . . King Faisal
'32, 34, 41 . Franklin D. Roosevelt	'75 . . . . American Women
'35 . . . . Haile Selassie	'76 . . . . Jimmy Carter
'36 . . . . Wallis Warfield Simpson	'77 . . . . Anwar Sadat
'38 . . . . Adolf Hitler	'78 . . . . Teng Hsiao-P'ing
'39, 42 . . . . Joseph Stalin	'79 . . . . Ayatullah Khomeini
'40, 49 . . . . Winston Churchill	'80 . . . . Ronald Reagan
'44, 59 . . . . Dwight D. Eisenhower	'81 . . . . Lech Walesa
'45, 48 . . . . Harry Truman	'82 . . . . The Computer
'50 . . . . American Fighting-Man	'83 . . . . Regan & Andropov
'52 . . . . Elizabeth II	'85 . . . . Deng Xiaoping
'55 . . . . Harlow Herbert Curtice	'87, 89 . . . . Mikhail Gorbachev
'56 . . . Hungarian Freedom Fighter	'88 . . . . Endangered Earth
'57 . . . . Nikita Krushchev	'90 . . . . The Two George Bushes
'58 . . . . Charles De Gaulle	'91 . . . . Ted Turner
'60 . . . . US Scientists	'92 . . . . Bill Clinton
'61 . . . . John F. Kennedy	'93 . . . . The Peacemakers
'62 . . . . Pope John XXIII	'94 . . . . Pope John Paul II
'63 . . . . Martin Luther King Jr.	'95 . . . . Newt Gingrich
'64, 67 . . . . Lyndon B. Johnson	'98 . Bill Clinton & Kenneth Starr
'66 . . . . Twenty-Five and Under	'99 . . . . Jeff Bezos
'68 . . . . . Anders, Borman, & Lovell	'00 . . . . George W. Bush
'69 . . . . The Middle Americans	'01 . . . . Rudy Giuliani
'71 . . . . Richard Millious Nixon	'02 . . . . The Whistle Blowers

———— FUJITA-PEARSON TORNADO ————
INTENSITY SCALE

MPH	F SCALE	DAMAGE	NAME
<73 . . . . F0 . . . . . *Damage to trees, signs, & chimneys* . . . . Gale
73–112 . . . . F1 . . . . *Roofs damaged; cars rocked* . . . . . Moderate
113–157 . . . . F2 . . . . *Roofs torn off; cars overturned* . . . . Significant
158–206 . . . . F3 . . . . *Forests uprooted; cars lifted* . . . . Severe
207–260 . . . . F4 . . . . . . *Homes destroyed; heavy objects fly* . . . Devastating
261–318 . . . . F5 . . . . . *Structures leveled; utter destruction* . . . . . Incredible
>319 . . . . F6 . . . . . . *Theoretical; not expected on Earth* . . . . ——

——DIANA, PRINCESS OF WALES' FUNERAL——

Below is given the Order of Service for the funeral of Diana, Princess of Wales, held in Westminster Abbey, at 11:00 a.m., on Saturday, September 6th, 1997.

MUSIC BEFORE THE SERVICE

2nd Movement, Organ Sonata, No.2
Felix Mendelssohn-Bartholdy

Prelude on the hymn tune Eventide
Hubert Parry

Adagio in E
Frank Bridge

Prelude on the hymn Rhosymedre
Ralph Vaughan Williams

Ich ruf zu dir, Herr Jesu Christ
Johann Sebastian Bach

Elegy
George Thalben-Ball

Fantasia in C minor
Johann Sebastian Bach

Adagio in G minor
Tomaso Giovanni Albinoni

*Slow movement, from the 9th
Symphony (From the New World)*
Antonin Dvořák

Canon
Johann Pachelbel

Nimrod
Edward Elgar

Prelude
William Harris

THE NATIONAL ANTHEM

THE SENTENCES

*I am the resurrection and the life,
saith the Lord: he that believeth in
me, though he were dead, yet shall he
live; and whosoever liveth and
believeth in me shall never die.*
(St John 11: 25,26)

*I know that my Redeemer liveth, and
that he shall stand at the latter day
upon the earth: and though after my
skin worms destroy this body, yet in
my flesh shall I see God; whom I shall
see for myself, and mine eyes shall
behold, and not another.*
(Job 19: 25-27)

*We brought nothing into this world,
and it is certain we can carry nothing
out. The Lord gave, and the Lord
hath taken away; blessed be the
name of the Lord.*
(1 Timothy 6: 7; Job 1: 21)

*Thou knowest, Lord, the secrets of our
hearts; shut not thy merciful ears unto
our prayer; but spare us, Lord most
holy, O God most mighty, O holy and
most merciful Savior, thou most
worthy Judge eternal, suffer us not, at
our last hour, for any pains of death,
to fall from thee. Amen*
(Book of Common Prayer)

*I heard a voice from heaven, saying
unto me, Write, From henceforth
blessed are the dead which die in the
Lord: even so saith the Spirit;
for they rest from their labors.*
(Revelation 14: 13)

───── PRINCESS OF WALES' FUNERAL cont. ─────

The Very Reverend Dr Wesley Carr,
Dean of Westminster
THE BIDDING

THE HYMN
I vow to thee, my country

Lady Sarah McCorquodale read
*If I should die and leave
you here awhile…*

BBC Singers, & Lynne Dawson
Libera me, Domine, de morte aeterna
Guiseppe Verdi

Lady Jane Fellowes read
Time is too slow for those who wait…

THE HYMN
The King of Love My Shepherd Is
J B Dykes

The Rt Hon Tony Blair, MP
Prime Minister, read
I CORINTHIANS XIII
*Though I speak with the tongues of
men and of angels…*

Elton John sang
Candle in the Wind

The Earl Spencer read
THE TRIBUTE

THE HYMN
Make me a channel of your peace

The Most Reverend and Right
Honourable Dr George Carey,
Lord Archbishop of Canterbury,
led
THE PRAYERS
for Diana, Princess of Wales

The choristers sang
*I would be true, for there are those
that trust me*
Air from County Derry in G

The Archbishop of Canterbury
THE LORD'S PRAYER

THE BLESSING

THE HYMN
Guide me, O thou great Redeemer
Cwm Rhondda
John Hughes

The Dean
THE COMMENDATION

As the Cortège left the church,
the Choir sang
*Alleluia. May flights of angels sing
thee to thy rest.*
John Tavener
*Extracts from Hamlet and the
Orthodox Funeral Service*

A MINUTE SILENCE

The half-muffled bells of
Westminster Abbey were rung

MUSIC AFTER THE SERVICE

Prelude in C minor
Johann Sebastian Bach

Maestoso, from Symphonie No.3.
Camille Saint-Saens

[*Sung by the Choir of Westminster Abbey,
conducted by Martin Neary.
The organist was Martin Baker,
Sub-Organist of Westminster Abbey.*]

---------------------- THE PLANETS ----------------------

Name	Diameter	No. of Moons	Surface Gravity	Rings?	Kms from Sun
MERCURY	4,878 km	0	370 cm/s²	no	57,909,175
VENUS	12,104	0	887	no	108,208,930
EARTH	12,756	1	980	no	149,597,890
MARS	6,794	2	371	no	227,936,640
JUPITER	142,800	39	2,312	yes	778,412,020
SATURN	120,536	30	896	yes	1,426,725,400
URANUS	51,118	20	869	yes	2,870,972,200
NEPTUNE	49,492	8	1,100	yes	4,498,252,900
PLUTO	2,300	1	81	no	5,906,376,200

---------------- BRITISH PASSPORT WORDING ----------------

*'Her Britannic Majesty's Principal Secretary of State [for Foreign and
Commonwealth Affairs] requests and requires in the name of Her Majesty
all those whom it may concern to allow the bearer to pass freely
without let or hindrance and to afford the bearer such
assistance and protection as may be necessary.'*

------------------- CONTRADICTANYMS -------------------

Contradictanyms are words which have opposing meanings depending
on the context in which they are used. For example, the word DUST can
mean to add fine particles (as in *dust the cake with icing sugar*) as well as
to remove fine particles (as in *dust the furniture*). Other examples include:

You must BOLT the door .... or he will BOLT for the door
FLOG a horse .... in order to FLOG the horse-meat
GARNISH that dish .... or I will GARNISH your earnings
Secure it with a BUCKLE .... or it will BUCKLE under the weight
Please SCREEN us from .... the film they are about to SCREEN
Though CRITICAL in his comments .... he was CRITICAL to our success
You can see the stars are OUT .... once the lights are OUT
It is everyday CUSTOM .... to have suits CUSTOM-made
It was an OVERSIGHT .... to give him OVERSIGHT of the project
I will FIX the gate .... in order to FIX the race
Bind him FAST to prevent .... a FAST getaway
He was only a QUALIFIED success .... although he is fully QUALIFIED

--------------- THE MOHS SCALE ---------------

In *c.* 1812, Austrian mineralogist F. Mohs developed a scale to compare the hardness of substances relative to a selection of 10 different minerals, each of which is harder and thus capable of scratching its predecessor:

[1] Talc · [2] Gypsum · [3] Calcite · [4] Fluorite · [5] Apatite
[6] Orthoclase · [7] Quartz · [8] Topaz · [9] Corundum · [10] Diamond

--------------- PANTAGRUEL'S LABORS ---------------

Rabelais' Gargantua demanded of his son Pantagruel the following toil:

❝ *I intend and insist that you learn all languages perfectly; first of all Greek, in Quintilian's method; then Latin, then Hebrew, then Arabic and Chaldee. I wish you to form your style of Greek on the model of Plato, and of Latin on that of Cicero. Let there be no history you have not at your fingers' ends, and study thoroughly cosmography and geography. Of liberal arts, such as geometry, mathematics, and music, I gave you a taste when not above five years old, and I would have you now master them fully. Study astronomy, but not divination and judicial astrology, which I consider mere vanities. As for civil law, I would have thee know the digests by heart. You should also have a perfect knowledge of the works of Nature, so that there is no sea, river, or smallest stream, which you do not know for what fish it is noted, whence it proceeds, and whither it directs its course; all fowls of the air, all shrubs and trees whether forest or orchard, all herbs and flowers, all metals and stones, should be mastered by you. Fail not at the same time most carefully to peruse the Talmudists and Cabalists, and be sure by frequent anatomies to gain a perfect knowledge of that other world called the microcosm, which is man. Master these in your young days, and let nothing be superficial; as you grow into manhood you must learn chivalry, warfare, and field maneuvers.* **❞**

------- ANTIQUARIAN BOOK ABBREVIATIONS -------

an	as new	dj	dust-jacket
f	fine: no defects	ep	endpapers
nf	near fine: slight wear	ge	gilt edges
vg	very good; some defects	htvb	Hors Texte, versos blank
g	good; average used book	insc	inscribed
ads	book includes advertisements	lp	large paper edition
aeg	all edges gilt	op	out of print
cl	cloth	rem	remainder
dec	decorated	teg	top edge gilt

—————————— A FOR 'ORSES ——————————

A........................... for 'orses	N........................... for lope
B .... for mutton	O......... for the wings of a dove
C........................... for miles	P.................... for ming seals
D.................... for dentures	Q...................... for snooker
E .... for ning paper	R........................... for mo
F..................... for vessence	S .... for midable
G...................... for police	T .... for two
H.................... for consent	U..................... for mizzam
I....................... for Novello	V...................... for victory
J...................... for oranges	W .... for quits
K........................ for teria	X..................... for breakfast
L.................... for leather	Y..................... for mistress
M .... for sis	Z.................... for breezes

————————— ATMOSPHERIC LAYERS —————————

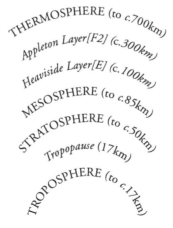

The Ozone Layer is located in the Stratosphere, between *c.*19–30km above the surface of the Earth. Ozone is created when energetic solar radiation strikes molecules of oxygen and causes the oxygen atoms to split apart. These atoms can then reform with O_2 molecules to form ozone (O_3): a process known as photolysis. Ozone absorbs the majority of solar UV radiation [290–400nm] some of which can be harmful to life on Earth.

SUMÓ

Bouts of *sumó* take place in the *dohyó* (ring) and are governed by the *gyóji* (referee) and five other judges. As befits a Japanese martial art, the ritual and courtesy of *sumó* are axiomatic. Wrestlers must be naked except for a *mawashi* (loincloth), 40cm wide, which is tied round the body in a series of precise moves. Each bout starts with complex standing, pledging, and purification movements, until the act of *tachiai* commences and the combatants rise to fight. A competitor loses the bout when any part of his body other than the soles of his feet touches the floor; when he is pushed from the boundary of the *dohyó*; or when he has performed *kinjite* (an illegal move). Illegal moves include slapping from the side, kicking, biting, and grabbing. In an attempt to qualify for recognition as an official Olympic sport, Sumó is adopting the following weight categories:

[♂] <85kg	....	LIGHT	....	<65kg [♀]
[♂] <115kg	....	MIDDLE	....	<80kg [♀]
[♂] >115kg	....	HEAVY	....	>80kg [♀]
[♂] unlimited	....	OPEN	....	unlimited [♀]

---

4 HORSEMEN OF THE APOCALYPSE

WAR *white horse* · SLAUGHTER *red horse*
FAMINE *black horse* · DEATH *pale horse*

PERSONAL AD ABBREVIATIONS

SOH............... sense of humor	SPARK... single parent raising kids
GSOH .... good sense of humor	NLP .... no losers please
WLTM......... would like to meet	NUMP......... no ugly men please
NTW............... no time wasters	WMP............... woo me please
LTR........ long-term relationship	ANI............. age not important
OHAC .... own house and car	GRO......... genuine replies only
PA........ photograph appreciated	NS .... non-smoker
ALA............ all letters answered	(A)NI .... (age) not important
BHM .... big handsome man	LTM .... longing to meet
SWF........... single white female	WTT............. willing to travel
SWM........... single white male	DTE............... down to earth
SBF............ single black female	FS..................... friendship
SBM .... single black male	ISO.................... in search of
SAF........... single Asian female	SD .... social drinker
SAM............ single Asian male	4TLC....... for tender loving care
DWM .... divorced white male	VGL............ very good looking

---

—————WINE BOTTLE NOMENCLATURE—————

Bottle Name	Champagne	Bordeaux	Burgundy
Picolo	¼	NA	NA
Chopine	NA	⅓	NA
Filette / Demi	½	½	½
Magnum	2	2	2
Marie Jeanne	NA	3	NA
Double Magnum	NA	4	NA
Jeroboam	4	6	4
Rehoboam	6	NA	6
Imperial	NA	8	NA
Methuselah	8	NA	8
Salmanazar	12	NA	12
Balthazar	16	16	16
Nebuchadnezzar	20	20	20
Melchior	24	24	24

Wine is usually matured in bottles no larger than a Magnum.

—————TECHNIQUES OF DIVINATION—————

observing facial features	anthroposcopy
analyzing currents of water	bletonism
studying the passage of smoke	capnomancy
behavior of birds	augury
looking into fire	pyromancy
examination of arrows	belomancy
interpreting oil poured on water	leconomancy
studying the entrails of animals	haruspicy
shadows or ghosts	sciomancy
examination of ashes	spodomancy
studying bones	osteomancy
analysis of numbers	arithmancy
interpretation of random (often biblical) texts	bibliomancy
becoming dizzy and falling	gyromancy
looking at fountains and springs	pegomancy
randomly drawing lots	sortilege
studying patterns in the flight of birds	ornithomancy
observation of lights or candles	lampadomancy
examining the entrails of sacrificial victims	hieroscopia
interpretation of laughter	geloscopy
burning straw on hot iron	sideromancy
analysis of pebbles	pessomancy

GLASGOW COMA SCALE

The Glasgow Coma Scale (GCS) was devised to help doctors assess the severity of head trauma and, importantly, to help track progress over time. The GCS is comprised of the sum of three tests: eye, verbal, and motor responses. The lowest possible GCS score is 3; the highest is 15.

BEST EYE RESPONSE
1 . . . . No eye opening
2 . . . . Eye opening to pain
3 . . . . Eye opening to speech
4 . . . . Eyes open spontaneously

BEST VERBAL RESPONSE
1 . . . . No verbal response
2 . . . . Incomprehensible sounds
3 . . . . Inappropriate words
4 . . . . Confused
5 . . . . Orientated

BEST MOTOR RESPONSE
1 . . . . No motor response
2 . . . . Extension to pain
3 . . . . Flexion to pain
4 . . . . Withdraws from pain
5 . . . . Localizes pain
6 . . . . Obeys commands

To provide medics with additional detail, the GCS is often expressed as its three components, for example:
GCS 9 = E2 V4 M3

EVENTS OF THE DECATHLON

first day – 100 meters · long jump · shot put · high jump · 400 meters
second day – 110-meter hurdles · discus throw · pole vault
javelin throw · 1500 meters

EUCLIDEAN AXIOMS & POSTULATES

Things equal to the same thing are also equal to one another.

If equals are added to equals, the sums are equal.

If equals are subtracted from equals, the remainders are equal.

Things that coincide with one another are equal to one another.

The whole is greater than a part.

It is possible to draw a straight line from any point to any other point.

Any straight line can be infinitely extended.

It is possible to describe a circle with any center and any radius.

All right angles are equal to one another.

If a straight line falling on two straight lines makes the interior angles on the same side less than two right angles, the straight lines, if produced indefinitely, will meet on that side on which the angles are less than the two right angles.

————————————— MI5, &c —————————————

The various British Military Intelligence units are the subject of much speculation, and only relatively recently have any MI departments been officially acknowledged. Some departments were only temporary, many have merged, others may be entirely apocryphal. A tentative list might be:

MI 1	Director of Military Intelligence; also cryptography
MI 2	Responsible for Russia and Scandinavia
MI 3	Responsible for Germany & Eastern Europe
MI 4	Aerial Reconnaissance during WWII
MI 5	Domestic intelligence and security
MI 6	Foreign intelligence and security
MI 8	Interception & interpretation of communications
MI 9	Clandestine operations · Escape and Evasion
MI 10	Weapons and technical analysis
MI 11	Field Security Police
MI 14	German specialists
MI 17	Secretariat body for MI departments
MI 19	POW debriefing unit

———————— PRESIDENTIAL ASSASSINATIONS ————————

LINCOLN *John Wilkes Booth* · GARFIELD *Charles J Guiteau*
McKINLEY *Leon Czolgosz* · KENNEDY *Lee Harvey Oswald (?)*

———————————— PATRON SAINTS ————————————

Barbers	St Louis	Tax collectors	St Matthew
Artists & creatives	St Luke	Broadcasters	St Gabriel
Cobblers	St Crispin	Horses	St Giles
Florists	St Dorothea	Dairymaids	St Brigid
Editors	St John Bosco	Taxi-drivers	St Fiacre
Sculptors	St Claude	Librarians	St Jerome
Tailors	St Homobonus	Pilgrims	St Mennas, St James
Wine growers	St Joseph	Singers	St Cecilia
Pin makers	St Sebastian	Invalids	St Roche
Lighthouse keepers	St Venerius	Bricklayers	St Stephen
Bee keepers	St Ambrose	Children	St Nicholas
Speleologists	St Benedict	Miners	St Barbara
Gravediggers	St Anthony	Syphilitics	St George
Bakers	St Honoratus	Hoteliers	St Armand, St Julien
Domestic servants	St Zita	Diplomats	St Gabriel

—SOME ACADEMY AWARD BEST PICTURES—

The following list tabulates some of the winners of the Best Picture award since its creation in 1928, and shows some of the competing nominees:

Year	Best Picture	Notable competition from
'33	CAVALCADE	*Little Women; 42nd Street*
'39	GONE WITH THE WIND	*The Wizard of Oz; Goodbye, Mr Chips*
'40	REBECCA	*The Grapes of Wrath; The Great Dictator*
'41	HOW GREEN WAS MY VALLEY	*Citizen Kane; The Maltese Falcon*
'42	MRS MINIVER	*The Magnificent Ambersons*
'46	THE BEST YEARS OF OUR LIVES	*It's a Wonderful Life*
'50	ALL ABOUT EVE	*Sunset Boulevard*
'61	WEST SIDE STORY	*The Hustler; The Guns of Navarone*
'62	LAWRENCE OF ARABIA	*To Kill a Mockingbird*
'64	MY FAIR LADY	*Dr Strangelove; Mary Poppins*
'67	IN THE HEAT OF THE NIGHT	*Bonnie and Clyde; The Graduate*
'70	PATTON	*M*A*S*H; Airport; Five Easy Pieces*
'71	THE FRENCH CONNECTION	*A Clockwork Orange*
'72	THE GODFATHER	*Cabaret; Deliverance*
'75	ONE FLEW OVER THE CUCKOO'S NEST	*Jaws; Nashville*
'76	ROCKY	*All the President's Men; Taxi Driver*
'77	ANNIE HALL	*Star Wars*
'79	KRAMER VS. KRAMER	*Apocalypse Now*
'80	ORDINARY PEOPLE	*Raging Bull; The Elephant Man*
'82	GANDHI	*E.T. The Extra-Terrestrial; Tootsie*
'84	AMADEUS	*The Killing Fields; A Passage to India*
'86	PLATOON	*Hannah and Her Sisters; The Mission*
'88	RAIN MAN	*Dangerous Liasons; The Accidental Tourist*
'89	DRIVING MISS DAISY	*Born on the 4th of July; Dead Poets' Society*
'90	DANCES WITH WOLVES	*Goodfellas; The Godfather, Part III*
'91	THE SILENCE OF THE LAMBS	*JFK*
'94	FORREST GUMP	*The Shawshank Redemption; Pulp Fiction*
'96	THE ENGLISH PATIENT	*Fargo; Shine; Jerry Maguire*
'97	TITANIC	*L.A. Confidential; As Good as it Gets*

—————SANDRINGHAM TIME—————

King Edward VII introduced the custom of setting the 180 or so clocks on the Sandringham Estate half an hour early to allow him more time to shoot. As a consequence, all business when the King was at Sandringham took place in this unique royal time zone. George V maintained this tradition, but Edward VIII, when he acceded to the throne in 1936, reset Sandringham's time pieces in synchronicity with the rest of his kingdom.

——— CATEGORIES OF NOMENCLATURE FOR ——— PLANET & SATELLITE FEATURES

Since 1919, the International Astronomical Union (IAU) has been responsible for the nomenclature of planets and satellites and their features. A complex taxonomy for naming new discoveries has developed providing thematic, historic, and even poetic associations with astronomical bodies. By convention, no names with military, political, or religious significance are allowed (excepting political figures alive before the 19thC), and no individual may be honored until they have been dead for at least three years. The following tabulation gives a few examples of categories used to name features on planets and satellites.

OBJECT	FEATURE	NOMENCLATURE CATEGORY
MOON	*Large craters*	Scholars, artists, and scientists
	Small craters	Common first names
VENUS	*Lineae*	Goddesses of war
	Dunes	Goddesses of deserts
	Terrae	Goddesses of love
MERCURY	*Valleys*	Radio-telescope facilities
MARS	*Large valleys*	Names for Mars in various languages
SATELLITES OF SATURN	*Tethys*	People and places in Homer's *Odyssey*
	Titan	Displaced ancient cultures
	Hyperion	Deities of the Sun and Moon
SATELLITES OF URANUS	*Miranda*	Characters and places from Shakespeare
	Titania	Female Shakespeare characters
EUROPA	*Rough terrain*	Places from Celtic mythology
	Ring features	Celtic stone circles

——————— BIRTHSTONES ———————

January	Garnet	July	Ruby
February	Amethyst	August	Sardonyx, Agate
March	Bloodstone	September	Sapphire
April	Diamond	October	Opal
May	Emerald	November	Topaz
June	Pearl, Alexandrite	December	Turquoise

SUSHI

Akagai	pepitona clam	Masu	trout
Anago	sea eel	Nori	sheets of dried seaweed
Aoyagi	Japanese red clam	Ocha	green tea
Ebi	boiled jumbo prawn	Saba	mackerel
Fugu	puffer fish	Sake	salmon
Gari	sliced ginger garnish	Sashimi	raw fish, without rice
Hamachi	yellowtail tuna	Shoyu	soy sauce
Hirame	halibut	Sushi	sweetened, pickled rice
Ika	squid	Tako	octopus
Ikura	salmon roe	Tamago	sweet, light omelette
Kaibashira	large scallops	Tekka Maki	tuna & rice roll
Kani	cooked crab	Toro	fatty tuna
Kappa	cucumber	Unagi	freshwater eel
Kobashira	small scallops	Uni	sea urchin
Maguro	tuna	Wasabi	hot Japanese horseradish

BAKER STREET IRREGULARS

The Baker Street Irregulars were Sherlock Holmes' 'unofficial force': a dozen London urchins, apparently headed by a boy named Wiggins. Holmes paid each boy a shilling a day, with a guinea prize to anyone who found the vital clue. Used by Holmes to search out information where he or the Police would be conspicuous, the Irregulars appeared in only three of the stories: *A Study In Scarlet, The Sign of Four,* and *The Crooked Man.*

OLYMPIC SWIMMING POOL SPECIFICATIONS

Length	50m	Lane width	2.5m
Width	25m	Water temperature	25–8°C
Number of lanes	8	Light intensity	>1500 lux

UN SECRETARIES-GENERAL

1946–52	Trygve Lie	*Norway*
1953–61	Dag Hammarskjöld	*Sweden*
1961–71	U Thant	*Burma*
1972–81	Kurt Waldheim	*Austria*
1982–91	Javier Pérez de Cuéllar	*Peru*
1992–96	Boutros Boutros-Ghali	*Egypt*
1997–	Kofi Annan	*Ghana*

─── PORTRAITS ON AMERICAN BANKNOTES ───

George Washington $1
Thomas Jefferson $2
Abraham Lincoln $5
Alexander Hamilton $10
Andrew Jackson $20
Ulysses S. Grant $50
Benjamin Franklin $100

OBSOLETE NOTES
William McKinley $500
Grover Cleveland $1,000
James Madison $5,000
Salmon P. Chase $10,000
Woodrow Wilson $100,000
[large bills used for Federal transactions]

─── CURIOUS DEATHS OF SOME BURMESE KINGS ───

THEINHKO killed by a farmer whose cucumbers he ate without permission (931 AD). Theinko's Queen, fearing civil disorder, smuggled the farmer into the royal palace and dressed him in royal robes. He was proclaimed King NYAUNG-U SAWRHAN, and was known as the 'Cucumber King'. He later transformed his cucumber plantation into a spacious and pleasant royal garden.

ANAWRAHTA gored by a buffalo during a military campaign. (1077)

UZANA trampled to death by an elephant. (1254)

NARATHIHAPATE forced at knife-point to take poison. (1287)

MINREKYAWSWA crushed to death by his own elephant. (1417)

RAZADARIT died after becoming entangled in the rope with which he was lassoing elephants. (1423)

TABINSHWETI beheaded by his chamberlains while searching for a fictitious white elephant. (1551)

NANDABAYIN laughed to death when informed, by a visiting Italian merchant, that Venice was a free state without a king. (1599)

─── THIN ICE ───

This table gives some idea of the theoretically 'safe' thickness of ice for different weights. Walking on any ice is absurdly dangerous: don't do it.

Load	Depth (")
Single person on skis	1.5
Single person on foot	2.5
Groups in single file	3
Snowmobile	3
Average car	7.5
Large car; small truck	8
Medium truck, 3.5 tons	9
7 tons	10
15 tons	15
25 tons	20
45 tons	25
70 tons	30

[The table assumes solid blue/black ice]

—— 'I LOVE YOU' ——

Afrikaans	Ek het jou lief
Arabic	Ohhe-buk
Braille	⠠⠊ ⠠⠇⠕⠧⠑ ⠠⠽⠕⠥
Burmese	Nin ko nga chitde; Chit pa de
Cantonese	Ngor oi ley
Catalan	T'estimo
Chewa	Noi makokonda; Ndimakukonda
Dutch	Ik hou van je
Esperanto	Mi amas vin
Finnish	Minä rakastan sinua
French	Je t'aime
Gaelic (Scot)	Tha gradh agam ort
German	Ich liebe dich
Ancient Greek	Se erotao
Gujarati	Maney tamari satey pyar che
Hawaiian	Aloha i'a au oe; Aloha au la o'e
Hebrew	Ani ohev otach
Hindi	Mai tumaha pyar karta hu
Italian	Ti amo
Japanese	Aishite imasu
Kurdish	Khoshim awée
Latin	Te amo
Lithuanian	As tave myliu
Morse	·· / ·−·· −−− ···− · / −·−− −−− ··−
Persian / Farsi	Mahn dousett daram; Ushegheh-tam
Pig Latin	Iway ovelay ouyay
Polish	Kocham cie
Portuguese	Eu te amo
Romanian	Te iubesc
Russian	Ya tebya lyublyu
Serbo-Croatian	Volim te; Ljubim te
Shona	Ndinoluda
Spanish	Te amo
Swedish	Jag älskar dig
Swiss German	I Chaa di Gärn
Tagalog	Iniibig kita; Mahal kita
Thai	Phom Rak Khun
Tswana	Keyagorata
Turkish	Seni seviyorum
Urdu	Mi-an aap say piyar karta hun
Welsh	'Rwy'n dy garu di
Yiddish	Ikh hob dikh lib
Zulu	Ngiya kuthanda

—————— AMERICAN DINER SLANG ——————

Adam 'n' Eve ... two poached eggs		gravel train............sugar bowl		
murphy...................potatoes		hemorrhage..............ketchup		
splash of red.........tomato soup		sea dust........................salt		
Adam's ale ....water		yum-yum....................sugar		
wreck 'em.......scramble the eggs		in the alley.....serve as a side dish		
moo juice.....................milk		java, joe.....................coffee		
belch water............soda water		life-preserver............doughnut		
on wheels....................to go		breath......................onions		
bucket of hail.........glass of ice		looseners..................prunes		

hounds on an island ....sausages on beans
put out the lights and cry ....liver and onions
bucket of cold mud ....bowl of chocolate ice cream
shingles with a shimmy ....toast and jam
two cows, make them cry ....two hamburgers with onions
zeppelins in a fog ....sausages in mashed potatoes

burn the British.... toasted muffin		lumber ....a toothpick		
clean up the kitchen..........hash		mike and ike ......salt and pepper		
on a raft...................on toast		no cow..............without milk		
wreath....................cabbage		sand...........................sugar		
bridge............four of anything		a squeeze.............orange juice		
hold the hail ....no ice		side-arms..........salt and pepper		
crowd............two of anything		warts........................olives		
Eve with a lid on........apple pie		axle grease..................butter		

——— SEVEN WONDERS OF THE ANCIENT WORLD ———

THE GREAT PYRAMID OF GIZA is the huge stone structure near the ancient city of Memphis, used as a tomb for the Egyptian Pharaoh Khufu.

THE HANGING GARDENS OF BABYLON built as part of the palace of King Nebuchadnezzar II on the banks of the Euphrates.

THE STATUE OF ZEUS AT OLYMPIA carved by the legendary sculptor Pheidias.

THE TEMPLE OF ARTEMIS AT EPHESUS built to honor the goddess of wilderness and hunting.

THE MAUSOLEUM AT HALICARNASSUS tomb constructed for King Maussollos, Persian satrap of Caria.

THE COLOSSUS OF RHODES giant statue of the sun-god Helios.

THE LIGHTHOUSE OF ALEXANDRIA built by the Ptolemies on the island of Pharos.

WORD PAIRINGS

floating wreckage	flotsam & jetsam	*items thrown off ships*
composer	Rodgers & Hammerstein	*lyricist*
elongated	Bert & Ernie	*rotund*
elbow flexor	biceps & triceps	*elbow extensor*
left-hand side facing forward	port & starboard	*right-hand side facing forward*
a high-range speaker	tweeter & woofer	*a bass-range speaker*
librettist	Gilbert & Sullivan	*composer*
destruction	rack & ruin	*destitution*
grey haired, grumpy	Statler & Waldorf	*white haired, grumpy*
lengthways	warp & weft	*crossways*
descends	stalactite & stalagmite	*ascends*
sea monster	Scylla & Charybdis	*whirlpool*
horizontal axis	x & y	*vertical axis*
svelte	Siskel & Ebert	*portly*
milk solids	curds & whey	*milk liquids*
movement up and down	pitch & yaw	*movement side to side*
linear gear	rack & pinion	*circular gear*
loquacious	Penn & Teller	*taciturn*

TRADITIONAL ALCOHOL MEASURES

BEER		SPIRITS	
nip	¼ pint	tot [whisky]	⅙ ⅕, ¼, or ⅓ gill
small	½ pint	noggin	1 gill
large	1 pint	bottle	1⅓ pints
flagon	1 quart	GILL	
anker	10 gallons	1 gill	¼ pint
tun	216 gallons	modern measures	25ml & 35ml

LAY vs MEDICAL TERMINOLOGY

Tummy rumbling	Borborygmi
Tennis elbow	Lateral epicondylitis
That thing at the back of the throat	Uvula
Athlete's foot	Tinea pedis
The ridge over the top lip	Philtrum
Fast pulse	Tachycardia
Housemaid's knee	Prepatellar bursitis
Squint	Strabismus
Bunions	Hallux valgus
That dent in the middle of the chest	Xiphisternum

————— IVY LEAGUE FIGHT SONGS —————

The phrase 'Ivy League' is said to have been coined by sports-writer Stanley Woodward in the 1930s. The league is made up of the following Colleges, each of which has a distinct sporting 'fight song':

STAND UP & CHEER (COLUMBIA)

Stand up and cheer / Stand up and cheer for old Columbia! / For today we raise / The Blue and White above the rest! / Our boys are fighting / And they are bound to win the fray / We've got the team! We've got the steam! / For this is old Columbia's day!

BULLDOG (YALE)

Bulldog, bulldog, bow-wow-wow, Eli Yale! / Bulldog, bulldog, bow-wow-wow, our team will never fail! / When the sons of Eli break through the line / That is the sign we hail / Bulldog, bulldog, bow-wow-wow, Eli Yale!

DARTMOUTH'S IN TOWN AGAIN

Dartmouth's in town again, Team! Team! Team! / Echo the old refrain, Team! Team! Team! / Dartmouth, for you we sing / Dartmouth, the echoes ring, / Dartmouth, we cheer for you! / Down where the men in Green, play on play / Are fighting like Dartmouth men / We have Dartmouth team, and say / Dartmouth's in town again!

FIGHT ON, PENNSYLVANIA

Fight on, Pennsylvania, put the ball across that line / Fight, you Pennsylvanians, there it goes across this time / Red and blue we're with you / And we're cheering for your men / So it's fight, fight, fight, Pennsylvan-I-a, / Fight on for Penn!

THE PRINCETON CANNON

In Princeton town we've got a team / That knows the way to play / With Princeton spirit back of them / They're sure to win the day / With cheers and song we'll rally round / The cannon as of yore / And Nassau's walls will echo with / The Princeton Tiger's roar: / And then we'll crash through that line of blue / And send the back on 'round the end! / Fight, fight for ev'ry yard, / Princeton's honor to defend. / Rah! Rah! Rah! / Rah! Tiger sis boom bah! / And locomotives by the score! / For we'll fight with a vim / That is dead sure to win / For Old Nassau.

GIVE MY REGARDS TO DAVY

Give my regards to Davy / Remember me to Tee Fee Crane / Tell all the pikers on the hill / That I'll be back again / Tell them just how I busted Lapping up the high highball / We'll all have drinks at Theodore Zinck's When I get back next fall! (CORNELL)

EVER TRUE TO BROWN

We are ever true to Brown / For we love our college dear / And wherever we may go / We are ready with a cheer / And the people always say / That you can't outshine Brown men / With their Rah! Rah! Rah! and their Ki! Yi! Yi! / And their B-R-O-W-N.

10,000 MEN OF HARVARD

Ten Thousand Men of Harvard want victory today / For they know that o'er old Eli / Fair Harvard holds sway / So then we'll conquer all old Eli's men / And when the game ends we'll sing again: / Ten thousand men of Harvard gained vict'ry today.

--------------- BRITISH WWII RATIONING ---------------

Rationing fluctuated throughout the war as the food supply changed. Below is the basic *weekly* ration for an adult in 1942, although this was supplemented by a system of monthly points for additional purchases.

MEAT . . . . to the value of 1*s*.2d.		SUGAR. 8oz, 225g	
BACON & HAM 4oz, 100g		TEA 2oz, 50g	
BUTTER. 2oz, 50g		EGGS 1	
CHEESE. 2–8oz, 50–225g		*Monthly Ration*	
MARGARINE. 4oz, 100g		PRESERVES. 1lb, 450g	
COOKING FAT 4oz, 100g		DRIED EGGS. 1pkt	
MILK. . . . . 2–3 pints		SWEETS 12oz, 350g	

--------------- WEDDING ANNIVERSARIES ---------------

YEAR	BRITISH	AMERICAN	MODERN
1st	Cotton	Paper	Clocks
2nd	Paper	Cotton	China
3rd	Leather	Leather	Crystal
4th	Fruit, Flowers	Linen, Silk	Appliances
5th	Wood	Wood	Silverware
6th	Sugar	Iron	Wooden
7th	Wool, Copper	Wool, Copper	Desk items
8th	Bronze, Pottery	Bronze	Linens, Lace
9th	Pottery, Willow	Pottery	Leather
10th	Tin	Tin, Aluminum	Diamond
11th	Steel	Steel	Jewellery
12th	Silk, Linen	Silk	Pearls
13th	Lace	Lace	Textiles, furs
14th	Ivory	Ivory	Gold
15th	Crystal	Crystal	Watches
20th	China	China	Platinum
25th	Silver	Silver	Sterling silver
30th	Pearl	Pearl	Diamond
35th	Coral	Coral, Jade	Jade
40th	Ruby	Ruby	Ruby
45th	Sapphire	Sapphire	Sapphire
50th	Gold	Gold	Gold
55th	Emerald	Emerald	Emerald
60th	Diamond	Diamond	Diamond
70th	Platinum	Platinum	Platinum
75th	Diamond	Diamond	Diamond

ANTIQUARIAN PAPER SIZES

BOOK SIZES

Name	*Inches*
Foolscap octavo	6¾ x 4¼
Crown octavo	7½ x 5
Large post octavo	8¼ x 5¼
Demy octavo	8¾ x 5⅝
Medium octavo	9 x 5¾
Royal octavo	10 x 6¼
Imperial octavo	11 x 7½
Foolscap quarto	8½ x 6¾
Crown quarto	10 x 7½
Demy quarto	11¼ x 8¾
Medium quarto	11½ x 9
Royal quarto	12½ x 10
Imperial quarto	15 x 11
Foolscap folio	13½ x 8½
Crown folio	15 x 10
Royal folio	20 x 12½
Imperial folio	22 x 15

WRITING PAPER SIZES

Emperor	66 x 47
Antiquarian	53 x 31
Grand Eagle	28¾ x 42
Double Elephant	40 x 26¾
Colombier	34½ x 23½
Atlas	34 x 26
Double Large Post	33 x 21
Double Demy	35½ x 22½
Double Post	30½ x 19
Imperial	30 x 22
Elephant	28 x 23
Super Royal	27 x 19
Double Foolscap	27 x 16½
Cartridge	26 x 21½
Royal	24 x 19
Medium	22 x 17½
Large Post	20¾ x 16½
Copy (Draught)	20 x 16
Demy	20 x 15½
Post	18¾ x 15¼
Pinched Post	18½ x 14¾
Foolscap	17 x 13½
Brief	16½ x 13¼
Pott	15 x 12½

THE BEAUFORT SCALE

Beaufort Scale	*Sea Height feet*	*Knots*	*MPH*	*Description*
0	—	<1	<1	Calm
1	¼	1–3	1–3	Light air
2	½	4–6	4–7	Light breeze
3	2	7–10	8–12	Gentle breeze
4	3½	11–16	13–18	Moderate breeze
5	6	17–21	19–24	Fresh breeze
6	9½	22–27	25–31	Strong breeze
7	13½	28–33	32–38	Near gale
8	18	34–40	39–46	Gale
9	23	41–47	47–54	Strong gale
10	29	48–55	55–63	Storm
11	37	56–63	64–72	Violent storm
12	—	≥64	≥73	Hurricane

—— PHOBIAS ——

Amphibians	batrachophobia
Beards	pogonophobia
Deformity	teratophobia
Fall of satellites	keraunothnetophobia
Being tied up	merinthophobia
Being contagious	tapinophobia
Theft	harpagophobia
Being stared at	ophthalmophobia
Tickling with feathers	pteronophobia
Sharks	selachophobia
Opening one's eyes	optophobia
Being touched	aphenphosmphobia
Blushing	ereuthophobia
Choking	pnigerophobia
Clowns	coulrophobia
Novelty	cainolophobia
Colors	chromatophobia
Detumescence	medomalacuphobia
Crossing bridges	gephyrophobia
Spiders	arachnophobia
Crowds	enochlophobia
Failure or defeat	kakorrhiaphobia
Being ridiculed	catagelophobia
Foreign languages	xenoglossophobia
Frogs	ranidaphobia
The skins of animals	doraphobia
Sea swell	cymobphobia
Garlic	scorodophobia
Getting wrinkles	rhytidophobia
Ghosts	phasmophobia
Going to school	didaskaleinophobia
Doctors	iatrophobia
Breezes	aurophobia
Gravity	barophobia
Hair	trichopathophobia
Hell	stygiophobia
Voids	kenophobia
Imperfection	atelophobia
Itching	acarophobia
Kissing	philematophobia
People or society	anthropophobia
Snow	chionophobia
Wasps	spheksophobia

PUBLIC SCHOOL SLANG

In his remarkable 1900 text, *The Public School Word Book*, John Farmer set out to collect 'words, phrases, names, and allusions to customs as are now, or have been, *peculiar* to English public school life'. The table below offers a small, and expurgated, selection of some of these curious phrases:

ABROAD *(Winchester)* Convalescing, out of the sick room.

ATHENS *(Eton)* A bathing place.

BAT-MUGGER *(Winchester)* Wooden instrument used to oil cricket bats.

BEARDS! *(The Leys)* An exclamation of surprise.

BIBBLING *(Winchester)* 6 cane strokes.

BOSTRUCHYZER *(Oxford)* A small comb for curling the whiskers.

CHARLIES *(Winchester)* Thick gloves made of twine.

CHEESE *(Cambridge)* A dandy.

CHINNER *(Winchester)* A wide grin.

CLIPE *(general)* To tell tales.

COXY *(general)* Stuck up, conceited.

DEVOR *(Charterhouse)* Plum cake.

DRY BOB *(Eton)* A cricketer.

EX TRUMPS *(Winchester)* Extempore.

FLUKE *(general)* To shirk.

GOD *(Eton)* 6th-form boy.

GROUT *(Marlborough)* To cram.

MAJOR *(general)* An older brother.

MINOR *(general)* A younger brother.

MUTTONER *(Winchester)* A blow on the knuckles while batting.

MUZZ *(Westminster)* To read.

NESTOR *(Eton)* An undersized boy.

NEW BUG *(general)* New boy.

ON & OFF *(Tonbridge)* Lemonade.

PEMPE *(Winchester)* Imaginary object that a NEW BUG is sent to find.

PEPPER *(general)* To mark in the accents on a Greek exercise.

QUILL *(Winchester)* To flatter.

ROD MAKER *(Winchester)* The man who makes the rods for BIBBLING.

SAPPY *(Durham)* Severe caning.

SWIPES *(Stonyhurst)* The boy who serves beer at supper.

TACK *(Sherborne)* A study feast.

TIZZYPOOLE *(general)* Fives ball.

WET BOB *(Eton)* A rower.

VARMINT *(general)* Good, smart.

THE HAMPTON COURT MAZE

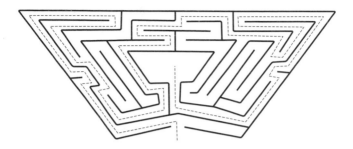

The maze at Hampton Court was planted sometime between 1689–95, by George London and Henry Wise, for William of Orange. It is thought the present design replaced an earlier maze of Wolsey's time. Originally constructed entirely from hornbeam, the maze has, over the years, been repaired and patched with a variety of different hedge types. Defoe called it 'a labyrinth', but really the maze is quite straightforward. As one writer noted, the maze 'is quite sufficient a puzzle to sustain interest and cause amusement, but without the needless and tedious excess of intricacy'. The maze occupies under ⅓ acre, and in total the walks stretch to about ½ mile.

GLOVE SIZES

Most traditional glove sizing dates back to the work of Grenoble-born Xavier Jouvin. In 1834, with the advent of accurate mechanised glove manufacture, Jouvin established a sizing system which was based on width of the knuckles. This system has survived metrification, and is still widely used, although there are differences between England and Europe:

| *English* | 6 | 6½ | 7 | 7½ | 8 | 8½ | 9 | 9½ | 10 |
| *Continental* | 6 | 7 | 8 | 9 | 10 | 11 | 12 | 13 | 14 |

The sleeve length of a glove is another consideration of sizing. Most gloves nowadays are worn very short, but for formal events much longer gloves are required. Sleeve length is often calculated by button length – a tradition which derives from the French technique of placing buttons an inch apart. So, a 4-button glove extends about 4 inches from the thumb. The following is a brief guide to the button lengths of some glove styles:

Shoulder length .... 20 | Elbow 8
Above elbow .... 16 | Mid-forearm 6

———— TWELVE DAYS OF CHRISTMAS ————

DAY	GIFTS FROM TRUE LOVE	CHRISTIAN INTERPRETATION
1st	A Partridge in a Pear Tree	*the One true God*
2nd	Two Turtle Doves	*the Old and New Testaments*
3rd	Three French Hens	*Faith, Hope, and Charity*
4th	Four Calling Birds	*the Four Gospels*
5th	Five Golden Rings	*the Books of Moses*
6th	Six Geese a-Laying	*the six Days of Creation*
7th	Seven Swans a-Swimming	*the seven gifts of the Holy Spirit*
8th	Eight Maids a-Milking	*the eight Beatitudes*
9th	Nine Ladies Dancing	*the nine Fruits of the Spirit*
10th	Ten Lords a-Leaping	*the Ten Commandments*
11th	Eleven Pipers Piping	*the eleven Faithful Apostles*
12th	Twelve Drummers Drumming	*the Apostles' Creed*

———— ARCHAIC GOLF CLUB NOMENCLATURE ————

Few formal links exist between modern and ancient golf clubs, but the list below gives an approximate guide to what comparisons can be made:

Woods No. 1 .... Play Club, Driver	No. 4 .... Jigger, Mashie Iron
No. 2 .... Brassie	No. 5 .... Mashie
No. 3 .... Spoon	No. 6 .... Spade Mashie
No. 4 .... Baffy	No. 7 .... Mashie-Niblick
	No. 8 .... Pitching Mashie
Irons No. 1.... Driving Iron, Cleek	No. 9 ...... Niblick, Baffing Spoon
No. 2 .... Cleek, Midiron	No. 10 .... Wedge or Jigger
No. 3 .... Mid-Mashie	Blank .... Putter

———— CHRONOGRAMS ————

Chronograms, or eteostichons, are inscriptions or riddles in which certain letters, representing Roman numerals, stand for dates. Perhaps the most famous chronogram is that written on the death of Queen Elizabeth I:

My Day Closed Is In Immortality = MDCIII = 1603

The Great Fire of London was marked with the following eteostichon:

LorD haVe MerCI Vpon Vs = L+D+V+M+C+I+V+V= 1666

Addison denounced chronograms as 'the results of monkish ignorance' and sneered that 'tricks in writing require much time and little capacity'.

--------------------- TONGUE TWISTERS ---------------------

Eleven benevolent elephants · Preshrunk silk-shirt sale
Three short sword sheaths · An Argyle Gargoyle
Gobbling gargoyles gobbled gabbling goblins
I wish to wash my Irish wristwatch · Lovely lemon liniment

--------------------- DEADMAN'S HAND ---------------------

James Butler 'Wild Bill' Hickock was a stockman, soldier, spy, deputy US
Marshall, multiple murderer, Sheriff of Ellis County, Ka., Marshall of
Abilene, Ka., and holder of the most famous hand in poker. When he was
shot dead by Jack McCall on August 2 1876, Wild Bill was holding two
black aces and two black eights – ever after known as 'Deadman's Hand'.

--------------------- YUPPIES ---------------------

BOBO . . . . Burnt Out But Opulent
BUPPIE . . . . Black Urban Professional
DINKIE . . . . Dual Income, No Kids
DINKY . . . . Double Income, No Kids (Yet)
DUMP . . . . Destitute Unemployed Mature Professional
GOLDIE . . . . Golden Oldie, Lives Dangerously
GUPPIE . . . . Gay Urban Professional
LOMBARD . . . . Lots Of Money But A Real Dickhead
NIMBY . . . . Not In My Back Yard
OINK . . . . One Income, No Kids
PIPPIE . . . . Person Inheriting Parents' Property
PUPPIE . . . . Poncy Urban Professional
SCUM . . . . Self-Centered Urban Male
SILKY . . . . Single Income, Loads of Kids
SINBAD . . . . Single Income, No Boyfriend, Absolutely Desperate
SINK . . . . Single, Independent, No Kids
SITCOM . . . . Single Income, Two Children, Outrageous Mortgage
WOOPIE . . . . Well-Off Older Person
YAPPIE . . . . Young Affluent Parent
YUPPIE . . . . Young Urban Professional Person

--------------------- THE FLAG OF KIRIBATI ---------------------

The top half is red, with a yellow frigate bird flying (right to left) over a
rising sun. The bottom half is dark blue with white waves forming a sea.

DEGREES OF FREEMASONRY

Freemasonry (a secret fraternal and semi-religious society) claims ancient lineage, and is said by some to employ the following 33-degree hierarchy:

1º	Entered Apprentice	1º
2º	Fellow Craft	2º
3º	Master Mason	3º
4º	Secret Master	4º
5º	Perfect Master	5º
6º	Intimate Secretary	6º
7º	Provost and Judge	7º
8º	Superintendent of the Building	8º
9º	Master Elect of Nine	9º
10º	Illustrious Master Elect of Fifteen	10º
11º	Sublime Knight, Chevalier Elect	11º
12º	Grand Master Architect	12º
13º	Royal Arch of Enoch	13º
14º	Scottish Knight of Perfection	14º
15º	Knight of the Sword & of The East	15º
16º	Prince of Jerusalem	16º
17º	Knight of the East & West	17º
18º	Knight of the Eagle & Pelican	18º
	and Sovereign Prince Rose Croix of Heredom	
19º	Grand Pontiff	19º
20º	Venerable Grand Master	20º
21º	Patriarch Noachite, Prussian Chevalier	21º
22º	Prince of Libanus, Royal Hatchet	22º
23º	Chief of the Tabernacle	23º
24º	Prince of the Tabernacle	24º
25º	Chevalier of the Brazen Serpent	25º
26º	Prince of Mercy	26º
27º	Grand Commander of the Temple	27º
28º	Knight of the Sun, Prince Adept	28º
29º	Knight of St Andrew	29º
30º	Grand Elected Knight Kadosh,	30º
	Knight of the Black and White Eagle	
31º	Grand Inspector Inquisitor Commander	31º
32º	Sublime Prince of the Royal Secret	32º
33º	Sovereign Grand Inspector General	33º

THE SEVEN DWARVES

Bashful · Doc · Dopey · Grumpy · Happy · Sleepy · Sneezy

KNIGHTS OF THE ROUND TABLE

According to Dryden, there were 12 knights; Sir Walter Scott named 16. The 10 given below seem to be accepted by most writers on the subject:

Lancelot · Tristram · Lamorack · Tor · Galahad
Gawain · Palomides · Kay · Mark · Mordred

ROMAN NUMERALS

1	I	30	XXX	600	DC
2	II	40	XL	700	DCC
3	III	50	L	800	DCCC
4	IV	60	LX	900	CM
5	V	70	LXX	1,000	M
6	VI	80	LXXX	5,000	$\overline{V}$
7	VII	90	XC	10,000	$\overline{X}$
8	VIII	100	C	50,000	$\overline{L}$
9	IX	200	CC	100,000	$\overline{C}$
10	X	400	CD	500,000	$\overline{D}$
20	XX	500	D	1,000,000	$\overline{M}$

THE APOSTLES

Simon (Peter) · Andrew · James · John · Philip · Bartholomew
Thomas (Didymus) · Matthew · James · Thaddaeus
Simon the Zealot · Judas Iscariot · Matthias

SYSTEMS OF GOVERNMENT

rule by	*is called*		*rule by*	*is called*
all equally	pantisocracy		the people	democracy
armed forces	militocracy		the poor	ptochocracy
bishops	exarchy		pope	paparchy
civil servants	bureaucracy		propertied class	timocracy
clerics	ecclesiarchy		religious law	theocracy
elderly	gerontocracy		saints	hagiarchy
eldest male	patriarchy		slaves	doulocracy
judges	kritarchy		a small cabal	oligarchy
men	androcracy		technical experts	technocracy
nobility	aristocracy		wealthy	plutocracy
one individual	autocracy		women	gynarchy
			the worst possible	kakistocracy

─────SOME TYPOGRAPHICAL TERMS─────

LEAD(ING) The spacing between baselines of text. Originally from the strip of soft metal separating lines of type.

KERN(ING) Overhang of one letter to another which affects the spacing of characters. Kerning is altered to make text more clear.

To   To
un-kerned   kerned

WORD SPACE The spacing added between words. This is usually equal when the right hand edge is ragged, but will vary when (as in this paragraph) the text is justified.

GUTTER Space between a number of columns, or between the text and the spine or edge.

DASHES There are three standard dashes: - (hyphen) – (en dash) — (em dash).

FONT TYPES sanserif, serif, *script*.

LETTERSPACING The spacing between the letters of a word, sometimes varied to improve legibility. It is not the same as KERNING (which affects pairs of letters), and should be used sparingly. It is normally employed only with uppercase titling text because, as Frederic Goudy once said, 'a man who would letterspace lowercase text would steal sheep'.

LIGATURES The conflation of two characters to avoid collisions or to facilitate legibility, for example:

fi rather than fi

LINE WEIGHTS ¼pt, ½ pt, 1–10pt

JUSTIFICATION The way in which text flows from left to right. Text can be left, right, or center justified or, like this paragraph, fully justified so that it runs flush against both the left and right margin.

TYPE STRUCTURE

TYPOGRAPHICAL POINT SIZES

4 5 6 7 8 9 10 11 12 14 18 24 36 48

INTERNATIONAL PAPER 'A' SIZES

A size	mm		
A10	26 x 37	A4	210 x 297
A9	37 x 52	A3	297 x 420
A8	52 x 74	A2	420 x 594
A7	74 x 105	A1	594 x 841
A6	105 x 148	A0	841 x 1189
A5	148 x 210	2A	1189 x 1682
		4A	1682 x 2378

HOW TO GET AN UPGRADE

Get an ink-stamp made from the
graphic shown and stamp it onto
the front of your airline tickets.
Seal the tickets in an envelope and
hand this over at the check-in desk
with an air of utter confidence.

VIP CUSTOMER UPGRADE WHEREVER POSSIBLE

DEWEY DECIMAL BOOK CLASSIFICATION

000–099	General works	500–599	Pure science
100–199	Philosophy	600–699	Technology
200–299	Religion	700–799	Arts
300–399	Social sciences	800–899	Literature
400–499	Language	900–999	Geography, History

395 Etiquette (Manners) · 399 Customs of war & diplomacy
441 French writing system & phonology · 648 Housekeeping
564 Fossil Mollusca & Molluscoidea · 624 Civil engineering
674 Lumber processing, wood products, cork

MONDAY'S CHILD

Monday's child is fair of face,
Tuesday's child is full of grace,
Wednesday's child is full of woe,
Thursday's child has far to go,
Friday's child is loving and giving,
Saturday's child works hard for his living,
And, the child that is born on the Sabbath day
is bonny, blithe, good, and gay.

POKER HANDS

1,098,240 ways	One pair	35 to 24
123,552 ways	Two pairs	20 to 1
54,912 ways	Three of a Kind	46 to 1
10,200 ways	Straight	254 to 1
5,108 ways	Flush	508 to 1
3,744 ways	Full House	693 to 1
624 ways	Four of a Kind	4,164 to 1
36 ways	Straight Flush	72,192 to 1
4 ways	Royal Flush	649,739 to 1

(The above table is based upon the premise that five cards are dealt.)

SGT. PEPPER

The following list contains some of those people whose images appeared on Peter Blake's celebrated 1967 cover of The Beatles' *Sgt. Pepper* album:

Aleister Crowley	Tony Curtis	Marlon Brando
Mae West	Wallace Berman	Tom Mix
Lenny Bruce	Tommy Handley	Albert Einstein
Karlheinz Stockhausen	Marilyn Monroe	Oscar Wilde
W.C. Fields	William Burroughs	Tyrone Power
Carl Gustav Jung	Richard Lindner	Larry Bell
Edgar Allan Poe	Oliver Hardy	Johnny Weissmuller
Fred Astaire	Karl Marx	Stephen Crane
Richard Merkin	H.G. Wells	Issy Bonn
Huntz Hall	Stuart Sutcliffe	Albert Stubbins
Simon Rodia	Dylan Thomas	Lewis Carroll
Bob Dylan	Dion	T.E. Lawrence
Aubrey Beardsley	David Livingstone	Sonny Liston
Sir Robert Peel	Stan Laurel	Marlene Dietrich
Aldous Huxley	George Bernard Shaw	Diana Dors
Terry Southern	Max Miller	Shirley Temple

THREE WISE MEN

MELCHIOR	King of Arabia	GOLD
CASPAR	King of Tarsus	FRANKINCENSE
BALTHAZAR	King of Ethiopia	MYRRH

'…and when they had opened their treasures, they presented unto him gifts: gold, and frankincense, and myrrh.' – Matthew 2:11

WWII POSTAL ACRONYMS

Traditionally, the following (somewhat louche) acronyms were written on the reverse of envelopes sent by soldiers to their lovers back at home.

B.U.R.M.A. . . . . Be Upstairs Ready My Angel
M.A.L.A.Y.A. . . . . My Ardent Lips Await Your Arrival
N.O.R.W.I.C.H. . . . . (K)nickers Off Ready When I Come Home
S.W.A.L.K. . . . . Sealed With A Loving Kiss
H.O.L.L.A.N.D. . . . . Hope Our Love Lasts And Never Dies
I.T.A.L.Y. . . . . I'm Thinking About Loving You
B.O.L.T.O.P . . . . Better On Lips Than On Paper

EMOTICONS

:-)	Hi, Smiling	{:-)	Wearing a toupee
;-)	Winking	+-:-)	The Pope
:-(	Frown	:-Q	Smoker
:-I	Indifferent	:-?	Pipe-smoker
>:->	Devilish	C=:-)	Chef
:-o	Wow!	@:-)	Wearing a turban
:-I	Grim	:-)8	Wearing a bow-tie
:-,	Smirking	!-(	Black eye
:-II	Angry	5:-)	Elvis
:-x	Kissing	:,(	Crying
:-"	Pursed lips	=):-)=	Abraham Lincoln
:-#	My lips are sealed	%-)	Dazed
8-I	Amazement	*<:-)	Santa
>-<	Absolutely livid!	0:-)	Angel
:-}	Mustached	:( )	Bigmouth
:*)	Drunk	:-#	Wearing braces
[:]	Robot	:-@	Screaming
8-)	Wearing sunglasses	:-Y	An aside
B:-)	Sunglasses on head	:-I :-I	Déjà vu
:-{}	Wearing lipstick	@}->--	Rose

SCORING CONKERS

As every schoolboy knows, conker players alternate striking their opponent's conker; each player receives three shots at a time. The game ends when one of the conkers is smashed. A conker is scored by the number of other conkers it has demolished. A new conker is always a 'one-er' – and its score increases by adding the score of its defeated opponent. For example, if a 'one-er' smashes another 'one-er' it becomes a 'two-er'. If a 'six-er' destroys a 'three-er' it becomes a 'nine-er' and so on.

THE ORDER OF ENGLISH SUCCESSION

The Bill of Rights 1689, and the Act of Settlement 1701, set down the order of Sucession to the English throne, and specified what conditions a new Sovereign must meet. Roman Catholics are specifically excluded from succession to the throne; and the Sovereign may not marry a Roman Catholic. The Sovereign must, additionally, be in communion with the Church of England, and must swear to preserve the established Churches of England and Scotland. The Sovereign must also swear to uphold the Protestant succession. The present order of Succession begins as follows:

The Prince of Wales · Prince William of Wales · Prince Henry of Wales
The Duke of York · Princess Beatrice of York · Princess Eugenie of York
The Earl of Wessex · The Princess Royal · Mr Peter Phillips
Miss Zara Phillips · Viscount Linley · Hon. Charles Armstrong-Jones
Hon. Margarita Armstrong-Jones · The Lady Sarah Chatto
Master Samuel Chatto · Master Arthur Chatto
The Duke of Gloucester · Earl of Ulster · The Lady Davina Windsor...

SOME 'Q' WORDS WITH NO 'U'

Qadi · Qanat · Qanon · Qasida · Qere · Qhat · Qi · Qiviut · Qwerty

THE PLEDGE OF ALLEGIANCE

According to Title 4, Chapter 1, Section 4 of the US Code, the Pledge of Allegiance should be made facing the flag, standing to attention, with the right hand over the heart. Men not in uniform should remove their headdress with their right hand and hold it at the left shoulder. Persons in uniform should remain silent, face the flag, and give the military salute.

*'I pledge allegiance to the flag of the United States of America
and to the Republic for which it stands, one nation,
under God, indivisible, with liberty and justice for all.'*

A Boston magazine, *The Youth's Companion,* first published the Pledge of Allegiance in 1892 to celebrate the 400th anniversary of America's discovery. However, the publication of the Pledge was not without controversy, since two writers for the *Companion,* James B. Upham and Francis Bellamy, both claimed authorship. A number of tribunals found in favour of Bellamy, and in 1957 the US Library of Congress confirmed his claim. In 1942, the Pledge was given official recognition by Congress; and, in 1954, the phrase 'under God' was added by Congressional decree.

MANUAL ALPHABET SIGNS

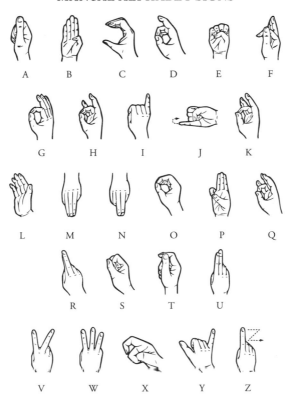

A B C D E F

G H I J K

L M N O P Q

R S T U

V W X Y Z

COLLEGES OF THE IVY LEAGUE

College	Location	Undergrads (c.)	Founded
Brown	Providence, Rhode Island	5,700	1764
Columbia	New York, New York	7,400	1754
Cornell	Ithaca, New York	13,300	1865
Dartmouth	Hanover, New Hampshire	4,200	1769
Harvard	Cambridge, Massachusetts	6,700	1636
Pennsylvania	Philadelphia, Pennsylvania	9,700	1740
Princeton	Princeton, New Jersey	4,600	1746
Yale	New Haven, Connecticut	5,200	1701

PALINDROMES

Sotades of Maronea (*c.*275BC) is credited as one of the early inventors of the palindrome: words or phrases that read the same backwards as forwards. Sotades is thought to have employed the device in many of his writings – writings that were often so obscene and defamatory that finally, having insulted Ptolemy II, he was encased in lead and drowned.

Sums are not set as a test on Erasmus[†]
Go deliver a dare, vile dog!
Madam, in Eden I'm Adam
May a moody baby doom a yam?
Do geese see God?
Murder for a jar of red rum
Never odd or even
Satan, oscillate my metallic sonatas!
Dogma: I am God
Ah, Satan sees Natasha
Norma is as selfless as I am, Ron[†]
Anne, I vote more cars race Rome to Vienna
Some men interpret nine memos
Are we not drawn onward, we few, drawn onward to new era?
Able was I, ere I saw Elba
Too bad — I hid a boot
A man, a plan, a canal: Panama

[†] *Indicates that the palindrome has been attributed to W.H. Auden*

THE ERINYES

Three daughters of Gaia, created from the blood of Uranus when he was castrated by Cronus, the Erinyes (or Furies) of Greek myth, were the spirits of conscience, punishment, and retribution. The three Erinyes are:

MEGAERA · *the jealous*
TISIPHONE · *the blood avenger*
ALECTO · *the unceasing*

The Erinyes are often represented in graphical form as winged goddesses with serpent hair, and eyes dripping blood. The Erinyes relentlessly pursued their victims until the guilty died in a furore of madness and remorse. So devastating was the power of the Erinyes that the Ancient Greeks dared not speak their real name for fear of provoking their wrath; instead they employed the euphemistic term Eumenides: the kindly ones.

————————— FAMOUS CAT & DOG OWNERS —————————

'I have had cats whom I liked better than this…but he is a very fine cat'[†]

SAMUEL JOHNSON[†]	Hodge
EDWARD LEAR	Foss
THE KENNEDYS	Tom Kitten
CHARLES DE GAULLE	Gris Gris
CARDINAL RICHELIEU	Perruque
SIMPSONS	Snowball II
DOWNING STREET	Humphrey
JOHN LENNON	Elvis
CHURCHILL	Margate, Jock
ALICE	Dinah
MARK TWAIN	Beelzebub
T.S. ELIOT	George Pushdragon
NICHOLAS I	Vashka

'Histories are more full of the examples of the fidelity of dogs than of friends'[‡]

ALEXANDER POPE[‡]	Bounce
GEORGE W. BUSH	Spotty, Barney
LORD BYRON	Boatswain
ISAAC NEWTON	Diamond
BILL CLINTON	Buddy
SIMPSONS	Santa's Little Helper
CHRISTOPHER MARLOWE	Bungey
HOGARTH	Trump
QUEEN ELIZABETH II	Susan[§]
JULES VERNE	Satellite
SPUTNIK II	Laika
MARTIN CRANE	Eddie

[§] *The Queen's 1st corgi; an 18th-birthday gift*

————————————— Pi —————————————

3.141592653589793238462643383279502884197169399375105
82097494459230781640628620899862803482534211706798821...

SOME CAPITAL CITIES

Andorra	Andorra la Vella
Angola	Luanda
Armenia	Yerevan
Azerbaijan	Baku
Bahamas	Nassau
Bahrain	Manama
Bangladesh	Dhaka
Barbados	Bridgetown
Belarus	Minsk
Belize	Belmopan
Benin	Porto-Novo
Bhutan	Thimphu
Botswana	Gaborone
Brazil	Brasília
Bulgaria	Sofia
Burkina Faso	Ouagadougou
Burundi	Bujumbura
Cambodia	Phnom Penh
Cape Verde	Praia
Chad	N'Djamena
Comoros	Moroni
Costa Rica	San José
Djibouti	Djibouti
Dominica	Roseau
Ecuador	Quito
Equatorial Guinea	Malabo
Eritrea	Asmara
Gabon	Libreville
Georgia	T'bilisi
Grenada	Saint George's
Guatemala	Guatemala City
Guinea	Conakry
Guinea-Bissau	Bissau
Guyana	Georgetown
Haiti	Port-au-Prince
Holy See	Vatican City
Honduras	Tegucigalpa
Indonesia	Jakarta
Kazakhstan	Astana
Kiribati	Tarawa
Kyrgyzstan	Bishkek
Laos	Vientiane
Latvia	Riga
Lesotho	Maseru
Liberia	Monrovia
Liechtenstein	Vaduz
Lithuania	Vilnius
Macedonia	Skopje
Madagascar	Antananarivo
Malawi	Lilongwe
Maldives	Male
Mali	Bamako
Marshall Islands	Majuro
Mauritania	Nouakchott
Mauritius	Port Louis
Moldova	Chisinau
Mongolia	Ulaanbaatar
Mozambique	Maputo
Namibia	Windhoek
Nauru	Yaren District
Niger	Niamey
Palau†	Koror
Panama	Panama City
Paraguay	Asunción
Portugal	Lisbon
Qatar	Doha
Rwanda	Kigali
Samoa	Apia
San Marino	San Marino
Saudi Arabia	Riyadh
Senegal	Dakar
Seychelles	Victoria
Sierra Leone	Freetown
Solomon Islands	Honiara
Somalia	Mogadishu
Sudan	Khartoum
Surinam	Paramaribo
Togo	Lomé
Tonga	Nuku'alofa
Turkmenistan	Ashgabat
Tuvalu	Funafuti Atoll
Uzbekistan	Tashkent
Vanuatu	Port-Vila
Zambia	Lusaka

† *A new capital for Palau is currently
under construction in Eastern Babelthuap.*

– 72 –

POLYGONS

3 sides	triangle	11	undecagon
4	quadrilateral	12	dodecagon
5	pentagon	13	tridecagon
6	hexagon	14	quadridecagon
7	heptagon	15	pentadecagon
8	octagon	16	hexadecagon
9	nonagon/enneagon	17	heptadecagon
10	decagon	18	octadecagon

SOME TONY BEST PLAY AWARDS

Some of the plays that have won the prestigious Best Play Tony award:

1949	Arthur Miller	Death of a Salesman
1950	T.S. Eliot	The Cocktail Party
1953	Arthur Miller	The Crucible
1956	Goodrich & Hackett	The Diary of Anne Frank
1957	Eugene O'Neill	Long Day's Journey Into Night
1962	Robert Bolt	A Man for All Seasons
1963	Edward Albee	Who's Afraid of Virginia Woolf
1967	Harold Pinter	The Homecoming
1970	Frank McMahon	Borstal Boy
1971	Anthony Shaffer	Sleuth
1975	Peter Shaffer	Equus
1976	Tom Stoppard	Travesties
1981	Peter Shaffer	Amadeus
1985	Neil Simon	Biloxi Blues
1990	Frank Galati	The Grapes of Wrath
1992	Brian Friel	Dancing at Lughnasa
1998	Yasmina Reza	Art
2000	Michael Frayn	Copenhagen

SOUND LEVELS – DECIBELS

0 db	Inaudible	90 .... City traffic, very annoying
10	Just audible	100 .... Firecrackers
30	Soft whisper (15ft)	110 .... Rock concert, power saw
40	Quiet office, living room	*– danger of permanent damage –*
60	Conversational speech	120 .... Car horn (3ft)
70	Noisy restaurant, intrusive	140 .... Air-raid siren, jet take-off
80	Hair-dryer, annoying	150 .... Rocket launch pad

CHAT ROOM ACRONYMS

LOVE & LUST

WTGP? . . . . want to go private?
BF / GF . . . . boy (girl) friend
H&K . . . . hugs and kisses
IWALU . . . . . I will always love you
DIKU? . . . . do I know you?
HAGN . . . . have a good night
ILY . . . . I love you
LJBF . . . . let's just be friends
SYT . . . . sweet young thing
FOAF . . . . friend of a friend
A/S/L? . . . . age/sex/location?
KOL . . . . kiss on lips
SO . . . . significant other
LY4E . . . . love you forever
SUAKM . . . . shut up and kiss me

TECHNICAL

RTBM . . . . . read the bloody manual
RTM . . . . read the manual
RYS . . . . read your screen
FAQ . . . . frequently asked questions
BRS . . . . big red switch
IRL . . . . in real life
MOTD . . . . message of the day
TPTB . . . . the powers that be
SLM . . . . see last mail
PDS . . . . please don't shout
TSR . . . . totally stupid rules
RHIP . . . . rank has its privileges

LAUGHING & CRYING

CSG . . . . chuckle, snicker, grin
LOL . . . . laughing out loud
BWL . . . . bursting with laughter
LMAO . . . . laughing my ass off
CID . . . . crying in disgrace
CRBT . . . . crying real big tears
SWL . . . . . . screaming with laughter
BEG . . . . big evil grin
ROFL . . . . rolling on floor laughing
JK . . . . just kidding
SICS . . . . sitting in chair snickering

ARGUMENTATIVE

BION . . . . believe it or not
AAMOF . . . . as a matter of fact
BOT . . . . back on topic
$0.02 . . . . my two cents
AFAIK . . . . as far as I know
PMBI . . . . pardon my butting in
IAAA . . . . I am an accountant
IAAL . . . . I am a lawyer
INPO . . . . in no particular order
FCOL . . . . for crying out loud
IOW . . . . in other words
GMTA . . . . . great minds think alike
OAUS . . . . . on an unrelated subject
IJWTS . . . . I just want to say
IMHO . . . . . in my humble opinion
IANALB . . . . I am not a lawyer, but
OTOH . . . . on the other hand
ITFA . . . . in the final analysis
PTMM . . . . please tell me more

MISCELLANEOUS

KISS . . . . keep it simple, stupid
AFK . . . . away from keyboard
NRN . . . . no reply necessary
FUD . . . . fear, uncertainty & doubt
12345 . . . . talk about school
BRB . . . . be right back
F2F . . . . face to face
BTW . . . . by the way
NQA . . . . no questions asked
YMMV . . . . . your mileage may vary
TANJ . . . . there ain't no justice
POV . . . . point of view
L8R G8R . . . . later 'gator
HTH . . . . hope that helps!
YGLT . . . . you're gonna love this
TYCLO . . . . turn your caps lock off!
LTNT . . . . long time, no type
SWIM . . . . see what I mean?
WAEF . . . . when all else fails
TOBAL . . . . . . there oughta be a law
NBD . . . . no big deal

———————— RYDER CUP RESULTS ————————

The Ryder Cup is a biennial golf tournament between the USA and Europe. First played between members of the British and US Professional Golfers' Associations in 1927, the cup itself was donated by British seed-merchant Samuel Ryder. In 1979 the British team was opened to Europeans, and in 1997 the European match was held outside Britain for the first time. The Cup was not contested during World War II, and the 2001 tournament was postponed for a year because of security concerns.

year	*winner*							
'02	Europe	'85	Europe	'67	USA	'49	USA
'99	USA	'83	USA	'65	USA	'47	USA
'97	Europe	'81	USA	'63	USA	– World War II –
'95	Europe	'79	USA	'61	USA	'37	USA
'93	USA	'77	USA	'59	USA	'35	USA
'91	USA	'75	USA	'57	Britain	'33	Britain
'89	tie	'73	USA	'55	USA	'31	USA
'87	Europe	'71	USA	'53	USA	'29	Britain
		'69	tie	'51	USA	'27	USA

———————— SOME SHAKESPEAREAN INSULTS ————————

You are not worth another word, else I'd call you Knave.

Why art thou then exasperate, thou idle immaterial skein of sleave-silk, thou green sarsenet flap for a sore eye, thou tassel of a prodigal's purse, thou? Ah, how the world is pestered with such waterflies, diminutives of nature.

Thou whoreson zed, thou unnecessary letter.

This woman's an easy glove, my Lord, she goes off and on at pleasure.

False of Heart, light of Ear, bloody handed, Hog in sloth, Fox in stealth, Wolf in greediness, Dog in madness, Lion in prey.

You shew'd your teethes like Apes, and fawn'd like hounds and bow'd like Bondmen.

Like the toad, ugly and venomous.

I would thou didst itch from head to foot and I had the scratching of thee; I would make thee the loathsomest scab in Greece.

You fat and greazy citizens.

Like a villaine with a smiling cheek, a goodly apple rotten at the heart.

You common cry of curs! whose breath I hate as reek o' th' rotten fens, whose loves I prize as the dead carcasses of unburied men that do corrupt my air.

—————— DECLARED NUCLEAR POWERS ——————

United States of America · Russia · China
United Kingdom · France · Pakistan · India · [Israel]

————— COMMONLY 'MISSPELED' WORDS —————

absence	diarrhea	mischievous	salary
accessible	disappearance	misspelled	separate
accidentally	drunkenness	mysterious	shining
acclaim	embarrass	necessary	skiing
aggravate	entrepreneur	obsolescent	soliloquy
alleged	existence	omelette	stubbornness
auxiliary	exuberance	origin	subtlety
basically	fascinate	parallel	success
because	fictitious	pastime	suddenness
beginning	forfeit	perseverance	surreptitious
believe	fulfilment	presumptuous	temperamental
biscuit	guarantee	pseudonym	tendency
broccoli	hindrance	pursue	tomorrow
business	idiosyncrasy	realistically	transferred
calendar	immediately	receive	truly
collectible	independent	recommend	twelfth
commitment	indispensable	remembrance	tyranny
connoisseur	inevitable	restaurant	unnecessary
conscientious	intelligence	rhythmical	until
consciousness	interesting	roommate	usage
corroborate	mediocre	sacrilegious	vacuum

————————— LETTER TRAITS —————————

No curved lines .... A·E·F·H·I·K·L·M·N·T·V·W·X·Y·Z
No straight lines... C·O·S
No enclosed areas............... C·E·F·G·H·I·J·K·L·M·N·S·T·U·V·W·X·Y·Z
Horizontal symmetry............................... B·C·D·E·H·I·K·O·X·
Vertical symmetry............................. A·H·I·M·O·T·U·V·W·X·Y
Roman numerals.. C·D·I·L·M·V·X
Just dots in Morse Code .... E·H·I·S
Just dashes in Morse Code .... M·O·T
Horizontal and vertical symmetry............................. H·I·O·X
Look the same upside down .... H·I·N·O·S·X·Z
Can be drawn in one stroke .... B·C·D·G·I·J·L·M·N·O·P·R·S·U·V·W·Z
Capitals which look like lowercase................... C·O·P·S·U·V·W·X·Z

—— YIDDISH ——

Billik	cheap, poor quality
Bobkes	worthless trifles
Bubbee	term of endearment
Chutzpah	nerve, brazenness, cheek
Danken Got!	thank God!
Drek	junk, rubbish
Frum	religiously devout
Gai avek!	go away
Gelt	money
Goy	a non-Jew, gentile
Kaddish	a prayer in mourning
Kibbitzer	interfering person
Klutz, Klotz	a clumsy person
K'vetsh	to whine or complain
Le'chayim!	the traditional toast 'to life'
Loch in kop	hole in the head
Mashugga, Meshughe	crazy, bonkers
Mazel Tov	congratulations, good luck!
Mieskeit	an ugly person or thing
Mitzveh	a good deed, a commandment
Naches	pride, joy [often that occasioned by children]
Nebbish	a nobody, a weakling or awkward person
Nosh	snack food; to snack
Nu?	so?
Nudnick	a pest, a bore; often a term of endearment
Oi!	all-purpose exclamation
Oi, gevald!	exclamation of torment
Schmuck, Shmock	dick
Shaitel	wig worn by Orthodox married women
Shalom	peace, a greeting
Shikseh	non-Jewish girl
Shlep (or Shlap)	to carry unwillingly
Shmaltzy	sentimental, sickly, corny
Shmendrik	a foolish, inept person
Shmoe	a naïve, easily deceived individual
Shmuts	dirt, mess
Shmutter, Shmatter	stuff, clutter, or a general term for cloth
Shnorrer	a beggar
Shtik	a special (theatrical) trick or turn
Shul	informal term for synagogue
Toches	ass
Traif	forbidden (non-kosher) food
Tsores	woe, troubles

EARTHQUAKE INTENSITY SCALES

RICHTER	MERCALLI SCALE & DESCRIPTION	SEVERITY
>4.3	I .... *Barely noticeable; doors may swing* II................. *Detected by some; slight* III.................... *Traffic-like vibration*	*Mild*
4.3–4.8	IV............... *Cars rock; pictures moved* V............ *Buildings tremble; trees shake*	*Moderate*
4.8–6.2	VI............ *Plaster cracks; hard to stand* VII ..... *Alarm; moderate building damage*	*Intermediate*
6.2–7.3	VIII .... *Fright; considerable damage* IX............ *Panic; landslides, earth shifts* X .... *Ground cracks; buildings collapse*	*Severe*
>7.3	XI .... *Destruction; few buildings stand* XII.... *Devastation; ground moves in waves*	*Catastrophic*

NATIONAL SPELLING BEE

Founded in 1925, the National Spelling Bee developed from an amalgamation of spelling competitions organized by local newspapers. Designed as a means of educating schoolchildren in the art of spelling, the National Spelling Bee is now run on a not-for-profit basis by The E.W. Scripps Company and over 240 sponsor companies. Some of the winning words at the annual National Spelling Bee Finals have included:

'26 .... abrogate	'62 ...... esquamulose	'91 .... antipyretic
'31............. foulard	'63.......... equipage	'92............. lyceum
'39 .... canonical	'67 .... chihuahua	'93 .... kamikaze
'42 .... sacrilegious	'68 .... abalone	'94 ...... antediluvian
'46........ semaphore	'79 .... maculature	'95 .... xanthosis
'49.......... dulcimer	'80 .... elucubrate	'96...... vivisepulture
'50 ...... meticulosity	'81....... sarcophagus	'97........... euonym
'51 .... insouciant	'82 .... psoriasis	'98 ..... chiaroscurist
'55 ..... crustaceology	'86........ odontalgia	'99 .... logorrhea
'57........... schappe	'87 ..... staphylococci	'00......... demarche
'58........... syllepsis	'89.......... spoliator	'01 ..... succedaneum
'61 .... smaragdine	'90 .... fibranne	'02 ...... prospicience

JOSEPH PULITZER

Hungarian-born Joseph Pulitzer (1847–1911), was a pioneer of popular and campaigning journalism. In his will he left $500,000 to endow the annual Pulitzer Prize for achievements in US journalism and literature.

THE IRISH CODE DUELLO

In 1777, during the Clonmell Summer Assizes, the Gentlemen delegates of Tipperary, Galway, Mayo, Sligo, and Roscommon prescribed a series of rules governing the practice of dueling and settling points of honor. It was recommended that 'Gentlemen throughout the Kingdom' should always keep a copy in their pistol cases, 'that ignorance might never be pleaded'.

1. The first offense requires the first apology, though the retort may have been more offensive than the insult.

4. When the *lie direct* is the *first* offense, the aggressor must either beg pardon in express terms, exchange two shots previous to apology, or three shots followed up by explanation; or fire on until a severe hit be received by one party or the other.

5. As a blow is strictly prohibited under any circumstances among Gentlemen, no verbal apology can be received for such an insult.

7. But no apology can be received, in any case, after the parties have actually taken their ground, without exchange of fires.

10. Any insult to a lady under a Gentleman's care or protection to be considered as, by one degree, a greater offense than if given to the gentleman personally, and to be regulated accordingly.

14. Seconds to be of equal rank in society with the principals they attend, inasmuch as a second may either choose or chance to become a principal, and *equality is indispensable.*

15. Challenges are never to be delivered at night, unless the party to be challenged intends leaving the place of offense before morning; for it is desirable to avoid all hot-headed proceedings.

16. The challenged has the right to choose his own weapon, unless the challenger gives his honor he is no swordsman; after which, however, he cannot decline any *second* species of weapon proposed by the challenger.

17. The challenged chooses his ground; the challenger chooses his distance; the seconds fix the time and terms of firing.

21. Seconds are bound to attempt a reconciliation *before* the meeting takes place, or *after* sufficient firing or hits, as specified.

22. Any wound sufficient to agitate the nerves and necessarily make the hand shake, must end the business for *that day.*

25. Where seconds disagree, and resolve to exchange shots themselves, it must be at the same time and at right angles with their principals. If with swords, side by side, with five paces interval.

ENGLISH MONARCHS

Danish Line

Svein Forkbeard.............. 1014
Canute the Great.......... 1017–35
Harald Harefoot........... 1035–40
Hardicanute 1040–42
Edward the Confessor..... 1042–66
Harold II...................... 1066

Norman Line

William the Conqueror ... 1066–87
William II Rufus 1087–1100
Henry I Beauclerc 1100–35
Stephen..................... 1135–54
Henry II Curtmantle 1154–89
Richard I the Lionheart ... 1189–99
John..................... 1199–1216
Henry III 1216–72
Edward I 1272–1307
Edward II................... 1307–27
Edward III 1327–77
Richard II.................. 1377–99

Plantagenet, Lancastrian Line

Henry IV 1399–1413
Henry V................... 1413–22
Henry VI 1422–61, 1470–71

Plantagenet, Yorkist Line

Edward IV 1461–70, 1471–83
Edward V 1483
Richard III Crookback..... 1483–85

House of Tudor

Henry VII Tudor 1485–1509
Henry VIII................. 1509–47
Edward VI 1547–53
Lady Jane Grey .... [9 days] 1553
Mary I Tudor 1553–8
Elizabeth I............... 1558–1603

House of Stuart

James I..................... 1603–25
Charles I................... 1625–49

Commonwealth

Oliver Cromwell 1649–58
Richard Cromwell......... 1658–59

House of Stuart, Restored

Charles II 1660–85
James II.................... 1685–88

House of Orange and Stuart

William III, Mary II 1689–1702

House of Stuart

Anne....................... 1702–14

House of Brunswick, Hanover

George I.................... 1714–27
George II 1727–60
George III 1760–1820
George IV.................. 1820–30
William IV................. 1830–37
Victoria.................. 1837–1901

House of Saxe-Coburg-Gotha

Edward VII 1901–10

House of Windsor

George V 1910–36
Edward VIII.................. 1936
George VI.................. 1936–52
Elizabeth II 1952–present

MONARCH MNEMONIC

Willy, Willy, Harry, Stee, Harry, Dick, John,
Harry III. I, II, III Neds, Richard II, Harrys
IV, V, VI... then who? Edwards IV, V, Dick
the bad, Harrys (twain) and Ned the Lad,
Mary, Bessie, James the vain, Charlie,
Charlie, James again... William & Mary,
Anne Gloria, Four Georges, William &
Victoria; Edward VII next & then George V
in 1910; Edward VIII soon abdicated:
George the VI was coronated; After which
Elizabeth, and that's the end until her death.

--------- PREFIXES ---------

10^{24}	yotta	Y	1 000 000 000 000 000 000 000 000
10^{21}	zetta	Z	1 000 000 000 000 000 000 000
10^{18}	exa	E	1 000 000 000 000 000 000
10^{15}	peta	P	1 000 000 000 000 000
10^{12}	tera	T	1 000 000 000 000
10^{9}	giga	G	1 000 000 000
10^{6}	mega	M	1 000 000
10^{3}	kilo	k	1 000
10^{2}	hecto	h	100
10	deca	da	10
1			1
10^{-1}	deci	d	0.1
10^{-2}	centi	c	0.01
10^{-3}	milli	m	0.001
10^{-6}	micro	u	0.000 001
10^{-9}	nano	n	0.000 000 001
10^{-12}	pico	p	0.000 000 000 001
10^{-15}	femto	f	0.000 000 000 000 001
10^{-18}	atto	a	0.000 000 000 000 000 001
10^{-21}	zepto	z	0.000 000 000 000 000 000 001
10^{-24}	yocto	y	0.000 000 000 000 000 000 000 001

--------- TWELVE LABORS OF HERCULES ---------

Killing the Nemean Lion
Killing the Hydra of Lerna
Capture of the Ceryneian Hind
Capture of the Erymanthian Boar
Cleaning the Stables of Augeas
Killing the Stymphalian Birds
Capturing the Cretan Bull
Capture the Mares of Diomedes
Acquisition of the Girdle of Hippolyte
Capture of the Cattle of Geryon
Acquisition of the Golden Apples of the Hesperides
Capture of Cerberus in the Underworld

--------- REINDEER ---------

Dasher · Dancer · Prancer · Vixen · Comet
Cupid · Donner (*or* Donder) · Blitzen · [Rudolph]

———————— BRITISH POETS LAUREATE ————————

The post of Poet Laureate probably dates back to the reign of Charles II, although prior to that poets, including Ben Jonson, were afforded royal patronage. Though nowadays the post has no formal obligations, most Laureates write on subjects of national interest, concern, and celebration.

1668–1688 . . . . John Dryden	1850–1892[‡] . Alfred, Lord Tennyson
1689–1692 . . . . . . Thomas Shadwell	1896–1913 . . . . Alfred Austin
1692–1715 . . . . Nahum Tate	1913–1930 . . . . Robert Bridges
1715–1718 . . . . Nicholas Rowe	1930–1967 . . . . John Masefield
1718–1730 . . . . Laurence Eusden	1968–1972 . . . . Cecil Day Lewis
1730–1757 . . . . Colley Cibber	1972–1984 . . . . . Sir John Betjeman
1757–1785[†] . . . . William Whitehead	1984–1998 . . . . Ted Hughes
1785–1790 . . . . Thomas Warton	1998– . . . . Andrew Motion
1790–1813[§] . . . . . . Henry James Pye	
1813–1843 . . . . Robert Southey	Laureate declined by: † Thomas Gray
1843–1850 . . . William Wordsworth	§ Walter Scott · ‡ Samuel Rogers

———————— THE TEN COMMANDMENTS ————————

[1] Thou shalt have no other Gods. [2] Thou shalt not make any graven images. [3] Thou shalt not take the Lord's name in vain. [4] Remember the Sabbath day. [5] Honor thy father and mother. [6] Thou shalt not kill. [7] Thou shalt not commit adultery. [8] Thou shalt not steal. [9] Thou shalt not bear false witness against thy neighbor. [10] Thou shalt not covet thy neighbor's house ... nor anything that is his.

———————— TV STANDARDS ————————

NTSC · *National Television System Committee*	. . . .	525 Lines/60Hz
PAL · *Phase Alternating Line*	. . . .	625 Lines/50Hz
SECAM · *Sequential Couleur Avec Mémoire*	. . . .	625 Lines/50Hz

———————— US PRESIDENTIAL INAUGURATION ————————

On the occasion of an inauguration, with their right hand raised aloft, and their left hand placed on an open Bible, the new President proclaims:

I do solemnly swear [or affirm] *that I will faithfully execute the office of President of the United States, and will, to the best of my ability, preserve, protect, and defend the Constitution of the United States.*

CRICKET FIELDING POSITIONS

KEY TO POSITIONS	i..........mid wicket	r................cover
a.......wicket keeper	j.....deep mid wicket	s ....point
b ....leg slip	k ....square leg	t...........silly point
c ....leg gully	l ......deep square leg	u.........silly mid off
d ....short square leg	m ....mid on	v.................gully
e ....short leg	n ....long on	w....slips (first–third)
f ....forward short leg	o ....mid off	x ....third man
g ....silly mid on	p ....long off	y ....fine leg
h....short mid wicket	q ....extra cover	z........deep fine leg

[Of course, this layout assumes that the batsman is right-handed.]

———— EURO NOTE SPECIFICATIONS ————

EUROS	COLOR	ARCHITECTURE	SIZE (MM)
5	Gray	Classical	120 x 62
10	Red	Romanesque	127 x 67
20	Blue	Gothic	133 x 72
50	Orange	Renaissance	140 x 77
100	Green	Rococo & Baroque	147 x 82
200	Brown	Iron & Glass	153 x 82
500	Purple	Modern	160 x 82

—— COLORS OF THE EMPIRE STATE BUILDING ——

New York's Empire State Building has a complex lighting system which allows the building to be colored in a variety of combinations. The lights are used to mark national holidays, charitable causes, ethnic celebrations, and the changes of season. The list below shows some of the color sequences and what they represent: *[Color sequence is from street level upwards]*

Red, Black, Green	Dr Martin Luther King, Jr. Day
Green	St Patrick's Day, March of Dimes, Earth Day
Red	St Valentine's Day, Fire Department Memorial Day
Red, Blue	Equal Parents Day, Children's Rights
Yellow, White	Spring, Easter Week
Blue, White, Blue	Israel Independence Day, Chanukah First Night
Blue	Police Memorial Day, Child-Abuse Prevention
Purple, White	Alzheimer's Awareness
Red, Yellow, Green	Portugal Day
Red, White, Blue	Flag Day, Presidents' Day, Armed Forces Day Memorial Day, Independence Day, Labor Day, Veterans' Day
Lavender, White	Stonewall Anniversary, Gay Pride
Purple, Teal, White	National Osteoporosis Society
Red, White, Green	Columbus Day
Blue, White	Greek Independence Day, United Nations Day
Black, Yellow, Red	German Reunification Day
Pink & White	Breast-Cancer Awareness
Red, Green	Holiday Season
No Lights	AIDS Awareness

On 4 June 2002, in a rare tribute to a foreign national, the Empire State Building was lit with the unique combination of Royal Purple and Gold to commemorate the Golden Jubilee of HM Queen Elizabeth II. Prior to this, the last non-American to be honored in light was Nelson Mandela.

EPONYMOUS FOODS

BEEF WELLINGTON *fillet steak wrapped in puff pastry* named to honor the Duke of Wellington.

PAVLOVA *meringue cake* named in honor of the acclaimed ballerina Anna Pavlova.

SAVARIN *rum-flavored fruit sponge* created by French chef, Antoine Brillat-Savarin.

EARL GREY *China tea infused with bergamot oil* favored and then popularized by Earl Grey.

FRANGIPANI *an almond-flavored cream* created by Marquis Muzio Frangipani.

APPLE CHARLOTTE *layered apple cake* named after Queen Charlotte, wife of George III.

SALLY LUNN *teacake* said to be created by Sally Lunn, a Bath pastry chef.

MOZARTKUGELN *marzipan with nougat cream, dipped in chocolate* created in Vienna in 1890 by Salzburg confectioner Paul Furst, and named in honor of Mozart.

GARIBALDI BISCUIT '*squashed-fly biscuits*' said to be named after Giuseppe Garibaldi, the Italian Nationalist, who liked them.

MADELEINE *light sponge cake* associated with Madeleine Palmier, a French pastry chef.

SACHERTORTE *rich layered chocolate cake* invented in Vienna by Franz Sacher.

PEACH MELBA *ice cream, peaches, and raspberry sauce* named after soprano Dame Nellie Melba, by Escoffier.

MELBA TOAST *toasted bread, sliced and baked* created at The Ritz to ameliorate Dame Nellie's diet.

THE SANDWICH named after the 4th Earl of Sandwich to facilitate simultaneous eating & gambling.

CHATEAUBRIAND *a deep cut of beef fillet* named after Ambassador Vicomte de Chateaubriand.

LADY GREY *Blended tea with orange & lemon peel, and bergamot oil* named after Lady Grey.

INTERNATIONAL ENVELOPE SIZES

Code	Size [mm]	Fits
C6	114 x 162	A6, A5 ½ folded
DL	110 x 220	A4 ⅓ folded
C6/5	114 x 229	A4 ⅓ folded
C5	162 x 229	A5, A4 ½ folded
C4	229 x 324	A4

Code	Size [mm]	Fits
C3	324 x 458	A3
B6	125 x 176	C6 envelope
B5	176 x 250	C5 envelope
B4	250 x 353	C4 envelope
E4	280 x 400	B4 envelope

BED SIZES

		IMPERIAL	METRIC cm
UK	(Small) Single	2'6" x 6'3"	75 x 190
	King (Standard) Single	3' x 6'3"	90 x 190
	Three Quarter	4' x 6'3"	120 x 190
	Double	4'6" x 6'3"	135 x 190
	King	5' x 6'3"	153 x 190
	Super King	6' x 6'6"	183 x 200
US	Twin/Single	3'3" x 6'3"	100 x 190
	Twin/Single extra long	3'3" x 6'8"	100 x 203
	Double/Full	4'6" x 6'3"	135 x 190
	Queen	5' x 6'8"	153 x 203
	King	6'6" x 6'8"	200 x 203
	California King	6' x 7'	183 x 213

Many versions of bed size exist; the above is an approximate guide only.

COMPOUND PLURALS

adjutants-general
aides-de-camp
ambassadors at large
attorneys at law
attorneys-general
billets-doux
bills of fare
bodies politic
brothers-in-law
changes of fortune
Chapels Royal
chargés d'affaires
chiefs of staff
coats of arms
commanders-in-chief
comptrollers-general
consuls-general

courts-martial
crêpes suzette
culs-de-sac
cupsful
daddies-long-legs
daughters-in-law
Doctors Who
editors-in-chief
filets mignons
fleurs-de-lis
gins and tonic
governors-general
grants-in-aid
heirs apparent
inspectors-general
knickerbockers glory
listeners-in

men-of-war
ministers-designate
mothers-in-law
passersby
pilots-in-command
Poets Laureate
postmasters-general
presidents-elect
prisoners of war
reductions in force
rights of way
secretaries-general
sergeants-at-arms
sergeants-major
solicitors-general
surgeons-general
trades union

WIVES OF HENRY VIII

Catherine of Aragon · Anne Boleyn · Jane Seymour
Anne of Cleves · Catherine Howard · Catherine Parr
[divorced, beheaded, died, divorced, beheaded, survived]

TUGS OF WAR

Specifications of competition-grade rope, as prescribed by
The Tug of War International Federation:

*'The rope must not be less than 10 centimetres (100 mm), or more than
12.5 centimetres (125 mm) in circumference, and must be free from knots
or other holdings for the hands. The ends of the rope shall have a whipping
finish. The minimum length of the rope must not be less than 33.5 metres.'*

HOW TO WRAP A SARI

THE NOBLE GASES

For some time thought to be inert, the Noble Gases are six highly stable
monoatomic gaseous elements which form Group 0 of the Periodic Table.

Helium (He) · Neon (Ne) · Argon (Ar)
Krypton (Kr) · Xenon (Xe) · Radon (Rn)

All of the Noble Gases were discovered by Sir William Ramsey, except
for Radon which was discovered by Fredrich Ernst Dorn.

———— RECORD SALES ————

SINGLES	*British Phonographic Industry*	ALBUMS

SINGLES		ALBUMS
200,000	Silver	60,000
400,000	Gold	100,000
600,000	Platinum	300,000

Recording Industry Association of America

500,000	Gold	500,000
1,000,000	Platinum	1,000,000
10,000,000	Diamond	10,000,000

——— FRENCH REVOLUTIONARY CALENDAR ———

The Revolutionary calendar was imposed on France by law on 5 October 1793. Dates were calculated from the Autumn Equinox, 22 September 1792, which became the first day of Year 1. The standard year was split into 12 thirty-day months with 5 (or 6) additional days (depending on leap years). The thirty-day months were named by the distinguished poet Fabre d'Eglantine, each month having its own appropriate symbolism:

Vendémiaire	vintage	*Germinal*	seed, budding
Brumaire	fog, mist	*Floréal*	blossom
Frimaire	frost	*Prairial*	meadow
Nivôse	snow	*Messidor*	harvest
Pluviôse	rain	*Thermidor*	heat
Ventôse	wind	*Fructidor*	fruits

Each of these months was subdivided into three *décades* of ten days: Primidi, Duodi, Tridi, Quartidi, Quintidi, Sextidi, Septidi, Octidi, Nonidi and Decadi, the day of rest. The remaining '*sans culottides*' were:

jour de la vertu	virtue day
jour du génie	genius day
jour du labour	labor day
jour de la raison	reason day
jour de la récompense	reward day
jour de la révolution	revolution day [leap years]

For obvious reasons, the calendar was unwieldy, impractical, and unpopular. Reforms were proposed, but instead Napoleon ordered the re-introduction of the traditional Gregorian calendar on 1 January 1806, thus condemning to death the Revolutionary calendar on 10 Nivôse XIV.

--- LATIN ABBREVS ---

AD	*Anno Domini*	in the year of our Lord
ad lib.	*ad libitum*	as much as you like
ad loc.	*ad locum*	indicating the place referred to
a.m.	*ante meridiem*	before noon
AMDG	*Ad Majorem Dei Gloriam*	to the greater glory of God
ca. or c.	*circa*	around
cf.	*confer*	compare with
DV	*Deo volente*	God willing
et al.	*et alii (et aliae, et alia)*	and other things
etc.	*etcetera*	and so on
fl.	*floruit*	the zenith of a person's life
ibid.	*ibidem*	in the same source
i.e.	*id est*	that is
loc. cit.	*loco citato*	in the place previously cited
MA	*Magister Artium*	master of arts
MD	*Medicinae Doctor*	doctor of medicine
MO	*modus operandi*	method of operating
NB	*nota bene*	note well
nem. con.	*nemine contradicente*	no one dissenting; unanimously
non seq.	*non sequitur*	it does not follow
op.	*opus*	piece of work
op. cit.	*opere citato*	in the work already mentioned
p.a.	*per annum*	each year
p.m.	*post meridiem*	afternoon
pp	*per pro*	(signed) on behalf of, in place of
pro tem.	*pro tempore*	for the time, temporarily
p.s.	*post scriptum*	written after
q.e.d	*quod erat demonstrandum*	thus proved
q.v.	*quod vide*	referring to text within a work
RIP	*requiescat in pace*	may he rest in peace
sic	*sic*	thus, or literally
v.	*vide*	see, look up
v. inf.	*vide infra*	see below
viz	*videlicet*	that is to say, namely
vox pop.	*vox populi*	voice of the people
vs.	*versus*	against

--- OPEC MEMBERS ---

Organization of the Petroleum Exporting Countries

Algeria · Indonesia · Iran · Iraq · Kuwait · Libya · Nigeria · Qatar
Saudi Arabia · United Arab Emirates · Venezuela

LLANFAIR PG · 53°13'N 4°12'W

The longest place name in Britain is said to be that of Anglesey village *Llanfairpwllgwyngyllgogerychwyrndrobwllllantysiliogogogoch* (58 letters) which translates as 'The church of St Mary in a hollow of white hazel near a rapid whirlpool and near St Tysilio's church by the red cave'. The name was invented in the nineteenth century as a lure to tourists.

ANIMAL AGES

According to Celtic legend

Thrice the age of a dog is that of a horse;
Thrice the age of a horse is that of a man;
Thrice the age of a man is that of a deer;
Thrice the age of a deer is that of an eagle.

VICTORIAN TIMETABLE OF FAMILY MOURNING

After the death of her beloved Albert in 1861, Queen Victoria set the standard for mourning. Befitting the age, outward displays were key: grief was represented on many levels, from the use of black-lined stationery and jet-black jewelry to elaborate funeral arrangements and periods of self-imposed social exile. Curiously, the period of mourning was decided not by personal sentiment but by a socially understood timetable of grief:

Death of	Period of mourning		
Husband	two to three years	Grandparents	six months
Wife	three months	Aunts & Uncles	three months
Parent or Child	one year	Nephews & Nieces	two months
Siblings	six months	Great Uncles & Aunts	six weeks
		First Cousins	four–six weeks

These individual mourning periods were themselves subdivided into first mourning, second mourning, ordinary, and half-mourning. By tradition first mourning was the deepest and lasted a year and a day. Each of these periods had its own subtle code – down to the shade of black, the types of cloth worn, and the width of hat-bands. Older children were expected to mourn alongside their parents, but often very young children were excused mourning dress. Servants' Mourning was normally considered appropriate after the death of a senior member of the household; when imposed, it usually lasted for at least six months. Never one to do things by half, Victoria wore mourning dress for the forty years until her death.

─────────────── NAVAL TIME KEEPING ───────────────

The traditional British naval watches are based on the following periods:

Time (24hr)	Watch		
00:00 – 04:00	*Middle Watch*	12:00 – 16:00	*Afternoon Watch*
04:00 – 08:00	*Morning Watch*	16:00 – 18:00	*First Dog Watch*
08:00 – 12:00	*Forenoon Watch*	18:00 – 20:00	*Last Dog Watch*
		20:00 – 00:00	*First Watch*

During the four-hour watches, bells are struck every half-hour in the following order. [To avoid confusion, bells are struck in pairs, with any odd bell struck afterwards: e.g. 5 bells would be *bell-bell / bell-bell / bell.*]

First half-hour	*1 bell*	Fifth half-hour	*5 bells*
First hour	*2 bells*	Third hour	*6 bells*
Third half-hour	*3 bells*	Seventh half-hour	*7 bells*
Second hour	*4 bells*	Fourth hour	*8 bells*

At the end of the First Dog Watch (18:00) 4 bells are struck (not the 8 that usually signify a change of watch). The Last Dog Watch bells are:

18:30	*1 bell*	19:30	*3 bells*
19:00	*2 bells*	20:00	*8 bells*

By tradition, 16 bells are struck to mark midnight on New Year's Eve.

─────────────── THE SEVEN SISTERS ───────────────

An informal term for the female equivalent of the Ivy League Colleges:

Barnard · Byrn Mawr · Mount Holyoke
Radcliffe · Smith · Vassar · Wellesley

─────────────── BOXING WEIGHT LIMITS ───────────────

Fighting class	limit (lbs)		
Straw weight	105	Lightweight	135
Junior Flyweight	108	Junior Welterweight	140
Flyweight	112	Welterweight	147
Junior Bantamweight	115	Junior Middleweight	154
Bantamweight	118	Middleweight	160
Junior Featherweight	122	Super Middleweight	168
Featherweight	126	Light Heavyweight	175
Junior Lightweight	130	Cruiserweight	190
		Heavyweight	unlimited

US NATIONAL FLORAL EMBLEM

'... we hold the rose dear as the symbol of life and love and devotion, of beauty and eternity. For the love of man and woman, for the love of mankind and God, for the love of country...'

With these words Ronald Reagan, on November 20 1986, proclaimed the rose to be the United States of America's 'National Floral Emblem'.

ORCHESTRA SCHEMATIC

PERCUSSION · TIMPANI

FRENCH HORNS · TRUMPETS · TROMBONES · TUBAS

CLARINETS · BASSOONS · CONTRA-BASSOONS

PICCOLOS · FLUTES · OBOES · CORS ANGLAIS

PIANO · HARP · FIRST VIOLINS · SECOND VIOLINS · VIOLAS · CELLOS · DOUBLE BASSES

CONDUCTOR

TUSSER ON THRIFTINESS

Tusser's 1557 poem *Thriftiness*, every word of which begins with a 't':

The thrifty that teacheth the thriving to thrive,
Teach timely to traverse, the thing that thou 'trive,
Transferring thy toiling, to timeliness taught,
This teacheth thee temp'rance, to temper thy thought,
Take Trusty (to trust to) that thinkest to thee,
That trustily thriftiness trowleth to thee.
Then temper thy travell, to tarry the tide;
This teacheth thee thriftiness, twenty times tryed,
Take thankfull thy talent, thank thankfully those
That thriftily teach thee thy time to transpose.
Troth twice to the teached, teach twenty times ten,
This trade thou that takest, take thrift to thee then.

——— SOME NAMED HAYDN SYMPHONIES ———

No.	Key	Name
22	E flat	The Philosopher
43	E flat	Mercury
45	F sharp minor	Farewell
48	C	Maria Theresia
55	E flat	The Schoolmaster
59	A	Fire
82	C	The Bear
83	G minor	The Hen
85	B flat	The Queen
94	G	The Surprise
96	D	The Miracle
100	G	The Military
103	E flat	The Drum Roll

——— SOME BALLET TERMS ———

CAMBRÉ · a bend from the waist.

CHANGEMENT · a jump where the position of the feet is changed.

ENCHAÎNEMENT · a series of steps linked together in a sequence.

ENTRECHAT · a jump where the legs criss-cross in the air.

FOUETTÉ · whipping move of the leg, often to create momentum to perform a turn or jump.

JETÉ · basic ballet step; a jump from one foot to the other.

PAS · a basic ballet step; often omitted as a prefix in ballet terms.

PAS DE DEUX · dance for two.

PAS DE QUATRE · dance for four.

PIROUETTE · a complete turn, or series of turns, on one leg.

PLIÉ · bending of the knees.

RELEVÉ · rising up off the heels.

SAUT · a jump off both feet landing in the same position.

SUR LES POINTES · on points.

TERRE À TERRE · steps where the feet hardly leave the ground.

VARIATION · a solo dance.

——— CANASTA SCORING ———

4s, 5s, 6s, 7s, 8s, 9s	5
10s, Js, Qs, Ks	10
2s, Aces	20
Jokers	50
Black 3s [where allowed]	5
Red 3s	100
All 4 Red 3s	800
Pure Canasta	500
Impure Canasta	300
Going out	100
Going out concealed	200

MINIMUM MELD VALUE TO GO DOWN

Negative score	15
Score of 0–1495	50
Score of 1500–2995	90
Score of >3000	120

———— COMMONPLACE GERMAN ————

Angst....................inner fear or torment, objectless anxiety
Bildungsroman..................novel describing personal development
Echt...real, genuine, authentic
Ersatz.......................................substitute, fake, imitation
Festschrift...........a commemorative publication to honor a colleague
Gedankenexperiment..............................thought experiment
Gemütlich....................................cosy, welcoming, pleasant
Gestalt.......................the overall shape or pattern of something
Götterdämmerung.. 'twilight of the Gods'; downfall of the once mighty
Hausfrau.............................house-wife [somewhat pejorative]
Hinterland......a private, personal space (usually outside of one's work)
Kaffeeklatsch..................................coffee culture, café society
Kitsch....................inauthentic, vulgar, tacky, derivative, or cheap
Leitmotiv..a recurring theme
Meister........................used as a suffix to mean expert, or master
Realpolitik..............................real-life, often cynical, politics
Schadenfreude............malicious pleasure in the misfortune of others
Schmalz...sickly sentimentality
Spiel...................................a glib, well-rehearsed patter
Sprachgefühl....................an intuitive ear for language and idiom
Sturm und Drang....Storm and Stress; late 18th-century romantic style
Urtext...original, authorized text
Verboten..forbidden, prohibited
Wanderlust...a yearning to travel
Weltanschauung.......................a worldview, a philosophy of life
Weltschmerz....................world weariness; despair with the world
Wunderkind..child prodigy
Zeitgeist...the spirit of the age

———— HERALDIC COLOR SYMBOLISM ————

Color	Symbolic Meaning	Associated Gemstone	Heraldic Name	Astrological Association
Black	Prudence	Diamond	Sable	Saturn
White	Innocence	Pearl	Argent	Luna
Red	Magnanimity	Ruby	Gules	Mars
Blue	Fidelity	Sapphire	Azure	Jupiter
Green	Love	Emerald	Vert	Venus
Yellow	Faith	Topaz	Or	Sol
Purple	Temperance	Amethyst	Purpure	Mercury
Tawny	Joy	Jacinth	Tenney	Dragon's head

SOME DEITIES OF VARIOUS CULTURES

EGYPTIAN

Ra . . . . sun
Khepera . . . . rising sun
Nut . . . . sky, heaven
Geb . . . . Earth
Hathor . . . . love, joy
Seth . . night, evil, turmoil
Horus . . . . light, all-seeing
Min . . . . fertility
Osiris . . . . life, underworld
Anubis . . . . lost, dead
Sekhmet . . . . wrath, might

JAPANESE

Ama-terasu . . . . Gods, sun
Kagutschi . . . . fire
Ebisu . . . . fisherman
Uzume . . . . happiness
Susanowa . . . . thunder
Tsuki-yumi . . . . moon
Wakahiru-me . . rising sun
Benten . . . . music, luck
Inari . . . . rice
Ukemochi . . food, fertility

NORSE

Odin . . . . Gods
Thor . . . . . thunder, crops
Freya . . . . . passion, beauty
Tyr . . . . battle, law
Loki . . . . mischief
Forseti . . . . justice
Hel . . . . underworld

HINDU

Brahma . . . . Creator
Vishnu . . . . Preserver
Shiva . . . . regeneration
Agni . . . . fire
Krishna . . . . love
Ganesh . . . . . wisdom, luck
Indra . . . . rain, thunder
Lakshmi . . beauty, fortune

GREEK	DEITY OF	ROMAN
Aphrodite	love	Venus
Hephaestus	fire	Vulcan
Apollo	light	Apollo
Poseidon	sea	Neptune
Ares	war	Mars
Hermes	travelers, thieves	Mercury
Artemis	hunting, fertility	Diana
Hades	underworld	Pluto
Asclepius	healing	Aesculapius
Dionysus	wine	Bacchus
Eros	love, desire	Cupid
Zeus	ruler of Gods	Jupiter
Nike	victory	Victoria
Amphitrite	sea, salt	Salacia
Eurus	east wind	Vulturus
Hestia	hearth, home	Vesta
Tyche	fortune	Fortuna
Pan	herds	Faunus
Palaemon	harbors	Portunus
Dike	justice	Astraea
Persephone	spring	Proserpina
Helios	sun	Sol
Alethia	truth	Veritas
Notus	south wind	Auster
Hebe	youth	Juventas
Eos	dawn	Aurora
Priapus	fecundity	Mutinus
Cronus	harvest	Saturnus
Selene	moon	Luna
Proteus	prophecy	Carmenta
Boreas	north wind	Aquilo
Enyo	war	Bellona
Eris	strife, discord	Discordia
Chloris	spring	Flora
Thanatos	death	Mors
Thalia	comedy	Comus
Athena	wisdom	Minerva
Gaea	the Earth	Terra
Hera	marriage	Juno
Hypnos	sleep	Somnus

There are wide variations in spelling. Also, some gods had influence in many spheres, often sharing powers with other deities.

COMMONPLACE LATIN

a posteriori . . . . reasoning or knowledge derived from experience
a priori . . . . reasoning or knowledge derived from first principles
alma mater . . . . nurturing mother [often old school or college]
alter ego . . . . other self; alternative personality
amor patriae . . . . love of country
annus mirabilis . . . . wonderful, remarkable year
apologia pro vita sua . . . . a justification of his life
ars longa, vita brevis . . . . art is long, life is short
casus belli . . . . the grounds of a dispute; an occasion for war
caveat emptor . . . . let the buyer beware
corpus delicti . . . . the evidence or body of a crime
cui bono? . . . . to whom good? who stands to gain?
de facto . . . . in reality; according to practice
de profundis . . . . out of the depths
et nunc et semper . . . . now and forever
ex cathedra . . . . an authoritative pronouncement
ex more . . . . according to custom
ex officio . . . . by virtue of one's office or position
ex post facto . . . . after the deed; retrospectively
flagrante delicto . . . . in the act of a crime
in loco parentis . . . . in place of a parent
in medias res . . . . into the middle of things
in vino veritas . . . . there is truth in wine; truth is spoken with wine
infra dig(nitatem) . . . . below one's dignity; lowering oneself
inter alia . . . . amongst other things
ipso facto . . . . by the fact itself
memento mori . . . . a reminder of death and mortality
mens sana in corpore sano . . . . a healthy mind in a healthy body
mutatis mutandis . . . . with the necessary changes having been made
ne plus ultra . . . . no more beyond; the zenith
(non) compos mentis . . . . (not) of sound mind
obiter dictum . . . . an incidental remark
passim . . . . everywhere, throughout
pax vobiscum . . . . peace be with you
persona non grata . . . . unwelcome, or unacceptable person
primus inter pares . . . . first among equals
pro patria . . . . for one's country
quis custodiet ipsos custodes? . . . . who watches the watchmen?
sine qua non . . . . without which nothing; a prerequisite
sub rosa . . . . communicated in secret
sui generis . . . . of its own kind, unique, a class alone
summa cum laude . . . . with highest praise
ultra vires . . . . beyond its legal authority

THE LANGUAGE OF FLOWERS

English Society learned a formal language of flowers from writers like Aubry de la Mottraye and Lady Mary Wortley Montagu, who brought back complex taxonomies of floral meanings from their travels abroad. Throughout the eighteenth and nineteenth centuries, a whole class of pale and listless ladies was preoccupied with the construction of subtle floral codes for their friends and admirers. A very few examples from these long and complex floral vocabularies are tabulated below:

Coquetry	Morning Glory	*Dangerous pleasures*	Tuberose
Concealed love	Acacia	*Curiosity*	Sycamore
You are cold	Hortensia	*Disdain*	Rue
Heart's ease	Pansy	*I am worthy of you*	White Rose
Ingratitude	Buttercups	*Perseverance*	Magnolia
Neglected beauty	Throatwood	*Foppery*	Coxcomb

Complementing this vocabulary was a specific grammar of floral arrangement. Flowers arranged on the left signified the sender, whereas those on the right represented the recipient. A flower presented upside-down would have its meaning reversed – so, a pansy set upright would signify 'heart's ease', but inverted would represent 'a distressed heart'. If the thorns of a flower were stripped it signified 'hope', but if the leaves were stripped it signified 'fear'. Numbers were denoted by an even more elaborate system of berries, leaves, and foliage. Thus, if a man wanted to present a subtle declaration of love to a girl on her 19th birthday he might present an evergreen wreath [*lasting as my affection*], with ten leaflets and nine berries [*19 years*], a red rose-bud [*pure and lovely*], ivy [*friendship*], and some peach-blossom [*I am your captive*]. This might then be gilded with periwinkle [*sweet remembrances*], and bachelor's-button [*love's hope*]

SOME EPONYMOUS WORDS

HANSARD (Parliamentary record)	Luke Hansard (1752–1828)
BUNSEN (burner)	Professor R.W. Bunsen (1811–99)
SAM BROWNE (army belt)	General Sir Samuel J. Browne (1824–1901)
BRAILLE	Louis Braille (1809–52)
SILHOUETTE	Etienne de Silhouette (1709–67)
BOWDLERIZE (to expurgate)	Thomas Bowdler (1754–1825)
QUISLING (traitor)	Vidkun Quisling (1887–1945)
SADISM	Marquis de Sade (1740–1814)
WELLINGTON (boot)	1st Duke of Wellington (1769–1852)
BOYCOTT	Captain Charles Cunningham Boycott (1832–97)
MANSARD (roof)	François Mansard (1598–1666)

—————— CHURCHILL & RHETORIC ——————

One of the greatest orators of the twentieth century, Winston Churchill understood the power of the tropes of classical rhetoric. The table below gives some rhetorical techniques, and provides Churchillian examples.

LITOTES
Deliberate understatement for dramatic or comic effect.
'Business carried on as usual during alterations on the map of Europe.'

PARADOX
A contradictory, but often revealing, logical anomaly.
'... decided only to be undecided, resolved to be irresolute, adamant for drift, solid for fluidity ...'

PARONOMASIA
Using similar-sounding words or phrases for effect.
'To jaw-jaw is always better than to war-war.'

PERIPHRASIS
Circuitously elaborate expression.
'... it cannot in the opinion of His Majesty's Government be classified as slavery in the extreme acceptance of the word without some risk of terminological inexactitude.'

CATACHRESIS
An unexpected image which stretches normal usage.
'a new Dark Age made more sinister ... by the lights of perverted science.'

EPIZEUXIS
Emphatic repetition.
'... this is the lesson: never give in, never give in, never, never, never, never ...'

EPISTROPHE / ANTISTROPHE
Repetition of words at the end of successive phrases.
'... the love of peace, the toil for peace, the strife for peace, the pursuit of peace ...'

ANTITHESIS
Juxtaposition of contrasting ideas with symmetrical phrasing.
'If we are together nothing is impossible, if we are divided all will fail.'

OXYMORON
The juxtaposition of two contradictory words or images.
'...an iron curtain has descended across the Continent.'

METONYMY
Use of a single term or image to represent a wider concept.
'We welcome Russia to her rightful place ... We welcome her flag upon the seas.'

CACOPHONY
Employment of harsh phrasing.
'that hideous apparatus of aggression which gashed Holland into ruin and slavery ...'

ANTIMETABOLE
Reversing the word order of a phrase previously employed.
'This is not the end. It is not even the beginning of the end. But it is, perhaps, the end of the beginning.'

CHURCHILL & RHETORIC cont.

SCESIS ONOMATON
Emphatic synonymous repetition.
*'Our difficulties and danger will
not be removed by closing our eyes
to them. They will not be removed
by mere waiting to see what
happens; nor will they be removed
by a policy of appeasement.'*

ASSONANCE & ALLITERATION
Repetition of vowel [assonance] and
consonant [alliteration] sounds.
*'Let it roll. Let it roll on full flood,
inexorable, irresistible, benignant,
to broader lands and better days.'*

BRACHYLOGIA
Abbreviated expression.
*'That was our constant fear: one
blow after another, terrible losses,
frightful dangers. Everything
miscarried.'*

ANAPHORA
Repetition of words or phrases at
the start of successive clauses.
*'We shall fight on the beaches. We
shall fight on the landing grounds.
We shall fight in the fields, and in
the streets, we shall fight in the hills.
We shall never surrender.'*

SHAKESPEARE'S PLAYS

Considerable debate still remains as to the chronology of Shakespeare's plays. The following is one account of the possible dates of composition:

The Comedy of Errors	1590[C]	Much Ado About Nothing	1599[C]
Titus Andronicus	1590[T]	Julius Caesar	1599[T]
The Taming of the Shrew	1591[C]	Twelfth Night	1600[C]
Henry VI Part 2	1591[H]	Hamlet	1601[T]
Henry VI Part 3	1591[H]	Troilus and Cressida	1602[C]
Henry VI Part 1	1592[H]	All's Well That Ends Well	1603[C]
Richard III	1592[H]	Measure for Measure	1604[C]
Love's Labour's Lost	1593[C]	Othello	1604[T]
Two Gentlemen of Verona	1593[C]	King Lear	1605[T]
A Midsummer Night's Dream	1594[C]	Macbeth	1605[T]
Romeo and Juliet	1595[T]	Antony and Cleopatra	1606[T]
Richard II	1595[H]	Timon of Athens	1606[T]
King John	1596[H]	Pericles, Prince of Tyre	1607[R]
The Merchant of Venice	1596[C]	Coriolanus	1608[T]
Henry IV Part 1	1597[H]	Cymbeline	1609[R]
The Merry Wives of Windsor	1597[C]	The Winter's Tale	1610[R]
Henry IV Part 2	1598[H]	The Tempest	1611[R]
As You Like It	1598[C]	Henry VIII	1613[H]
Henry V	1599[H]	(Two Noble Kinsmen)	1613[C]

Key: [C]omedy · [T]ragedy · [H]istory · [R]omance

ZODIAC DATES

F	♈	Aries .... March 21 – April 20 .... Ram	♂
E	♉	Taurus........... April 21 – May 21 .... Bull	♀
A	♊	Gemini........... May 22 – June 21 .... Twins	♂
W	♋	Cancer .... June 22 – July 23 .... Crab	♀
F	♌	Leo .... July 24 – August 23 .... Lion	♂
E	♍	Virgo .... August 24 – September 23.......... Virgin	♀
A	♎	Libra........ September 24 – October 23.............. Scales	♂
W	♏	Scorpio........ October 24 – November 22....... Scorpion	♀
F	♐	Sagittarius .. November 23 – December 22.......... Archer	♂
E	♑	Capricorn ... December 23 – January 20 .... Goat	♀
A	♒	Aquarius ...... January 21 – February 19..... Water Carrier	♂
W	♓	Pisces........ February 20 – March 20 .... Fish	♀

[*Dates change from year to year.*] · ^{F}ire · ^{E}arth · ^{A}ir · ^{W}ater · ♂ masculine · ♀ feminine

COUNTRIES IN THE EURO ZONE

Euro notes and coins were introduced in twelve member states of the European Unionon on 1 January 2002 ('E-day'). The countries in this first phase of the Euro are shown below, along with the names and codes of their old currency, and the irrevocable conversion rates which were calculated on 1 January 1999. Since the introduction of the Euro, the US Dollar has been worth approximately 1 Euro — though rates fluctuate.

COUNTRY	OLD CURRENCY	CONVERSION	OLD CODE
Austria	*Schilling*	13.7603	ATS
Belgium	*Franc*	40.3399	BEF
Germany	*Mark*	1.95583..............	DEM
Spain	*Peseta*	166.386	ESP
The Netherlands	*Guilder*	2.20371	NLG
Finland	*Markka*.................	5.94573	FIM
France..............	*Franc*	6.55957	FRF
Ireland.............	*Punt*	0.787564	IEP
Italy	*Lira*.	1936.27..............	ITL
Luxembourg.........	*Franc*	40.3399..............	LUF
Portugal	*Escudo*	200.482	PTE
Greece..............	*Drachma*.	340.750	GRD

DRACONIAN

The term *Draconian* derives from DRACO, the Archon at Athens *c.*621BC. Draco's laws, 'written in blood', prescribed death for even trivial crimes.

CLOUD TYPES

CIRRUS
[Ci] 5000–13700m
High, detached, white filaments or fibers of delicate, wispy cloud.

CIRROCUMULUS
[Cc] 5000–13700m
'Mackerel sky' – grains or ripples of white cloud in regular patterns.

CIRROSTRATUS
[Cs] 5000–13700m
Sheets of cloud covering much of sky, sometimes giving a 'halo' effect.

ALTOCUMULUS
[Ac] 2000–7000m
Patches and sheets of rounded or rolled cloud – separate or merged.

ALTOSTRATUS
[As] 2000–7000m
Sheets of gray-blue cloud covering the sky, often obscuring sun & moon.

NIMBOSTRATUS
[Ns] 900–3000m
Associated with rain & snow, covers most of the sky; dark and heavy.

STRATOCUMULUS
[Sc] 460–2000m
Layers of white cloud with dark gray areas; often light rain or snow.

STRATUS
[St] surface–460m
Uniform gray cloud, outline of sun & moon visible if cloud is thin.

CUMULUS
[Cu] 460–2000m
Heaped, cauliflower shape; brilliant white areas with dark bases.

CUMULONIMBUS
[Cb] 460–2000m
Heavy, dense cloud with huge tall towers and dark shadows at base.

In his essay 'On the Modification of Clouds', Luke Howard (1772–1864) employed four Latin terms to categorize the clouds he saw around him; these terms still form the basis of modern cloud taxonomy: cumulus, heap · stratus, layer · cirrus, curl · nimbus, rain.

———————— MULTIPLE NOBEL PRIZE WINNERS ————————

The Nobel Prize is the bequest of Alfred Nobel (1833–96), the inventor of dynamite. Since 1901, prizes have been awarded annually for significant achievements in chemistry, physics, medicine, literature, and peace. Very few people, or organizations, have been awarded more than one prize:

MARIE CURIE
1903 *Physics* · 1911 *Chemistry*

LINUS PAULING
1954 *Chemistry* · 1962 *Peace*

UN HIGH COMMISSION
FOR REFUGEES
1954 *Peace* · 1981 *Peace*

THE RED CROSS
1917 *Peace* · 1944 *Peace*
1963 *Peace*

FREDERICK SANGER
1958 *Chemistry* · 1980 *Chemistry*

JOHN BARDEEN
1956 *Physics* · 1972 *Physics*

———————— WORDS WITH ALL THE VOWELS IN ————————
ALPHABETICAL ORDER

Abstemious · Abstentious · Arsenious · Caesious · Facetious · Fracedinous

———————————— PENCIL HARDNESS ————————————

The process of determining pencil hardness dates back to the work of Nicolas-Jacques Conté, who (*c.*1795) developed techniques for controlling the ratio of clay to graphite in pencil manufacture. The Conté grading system was a numerical scale where 1 was the hardest and 4 the softest. Later, British manufacturers developed their own letter-based grading system with softer leads given a B (for 'black') preface, and harder leads prefaced H (for 'hard'). Over time, these two scales have been combined to create a scale used widely across Europe and occasionally in America:

hardest — 9H, 8H, 7H … 2H, H, F, HB, B, 2B … 7B, 8B, 9B — *softest*

Many US pencil manufacturers, however, use a numerical code which inverts Conté's gradings, making #1 the softest, and #4 the hardest. A rough chart of equivalence between the two systems can be shown thus:

softest — #1 = B, #2 = HB, #2½ = F, #3 = H, #4 = 2H — *hardest*

All of these grading systems are to some extent arbitrary, since no strict or formal definitions of pencil hardness have ever been universally adopted.

CONVERSIONS ANCIENT & MODERN

CAPACITY

Scotch pint ...... 105 cubic inches
Barrel of soap .... 256 lbs
Barrel of herrings .... 32 lbs
Tub of butter .... 84 lbs
Soldier's canteen .... 3 pints
Gallipoli oil Salma .... 14.232 gills
Bordeaux Barreque ..... 51.61 gills
Cadiz Fanega .... 1.55 bushels
Trieste Stajo .... 0.691 bushels
Scotch Boll .... 1 English sack

WEIGHT

24 grains .... 1 pennyweight
Drop .... 1 grain
Bale .... 90 lbs
12 sacks .... 1 last
Last .... 39 cwt
Truss of hay .... 60 lbs
Man's load .... 5 bushels
Market load .... 40 bushels
Naples Picollo .... 7420 grains
Bengal Maund .... 120 lbs
Bazar Maund .... 82 lbs
Mysore Cutcha Seer .... 9 oz
Seam of glass .... 120 lbs
Bassora Biscal .... 72 grains
Chaldron .... 28 cwt

BIBLICAL MEASURES

Cubitt .... 21.8"
Omer .... 0.45 peck
Ephan .... 10 omers
Schekel .... 14.1 grams

LENGTH

48 hair's-breadths .... 1"
3 barleycorns (lengthways) ...... 1"
Nail .... 2½"
Hand .... 4"
Palm .... 3"
Span .... 9"
Pole .... 5½ yards
Fathom .... 6'
Pace .... 4'4"
French Toise .... 6.395'
Guinean Jacktam .... 4 yards
Chinese Covid .... 14.62"
Indian Candi .... 2'1"
Levantine Pig .... 2'4"
Jaghire .... 10.46"
Greek Studium .... 600'
Olympic Foot .... 12¾"
Greek Acaena .... 10 foot-rod
Chain .... 4 poles
Ox gang .... 15 acres
Hide of land .... 100–120 acres

MODERN CONVERSION MULTIPLICATIONS

IMPERIAL	imperial to metric multiply by	metric to imperial multiply by	METRIC
inches	2.54	0.3937	centimeters
feet	0.3048	3.2808	meters
yards	0.9144	1.0936	meters
miles	1.6093	0.6214	kilometers
acres	0.4047	2.471	hectares
square miles	2.5899	0.386	square kilometers
US pints (liquid)	0.4731	2.1134	liters
US gallons (liquid)	3.7854	0.2641	liters
pounds	0.4536	2.2046	kilograms
tons (long)	1.016	0.9842	tons (metric)

———— ART STYLES: GOTHIC TO CUBISM ————

GOTHIC (12th–16thC) Detailed & devotional: pointed stone arches, stained glass and ribbed vaulting. (16thC) INTERNATIONAL GOTHIC Late-medieval art style. [*Pisanello*]

RENAISSANCE (14th–16thC) The classical revival in learning & all manner of sculpture, art, and architecture. Oil painting and use of perspective were developed. [*Botticelli, da Vinci, Ghiberti*]

MANNERISM (mid–late 16thC) An exaggeration of the Renaissance, which grew overly extravagant and stylised. [*Michelangelo, Bronzino*]

BAROQUE (17thC) Encouraged by the Roman Catholic Church, the Baroque style unified the various forms of art and architecture, creating realistic & dramatic work. [*Caravaggio, Bernini, Rubens*]

ROCOCO (mid–late 18thC) A highly ornate and lightweight, decorative style, developed in part at the elaborate court of King Louis XV. [*Watteau, Fragonard, Tiepolo*]

NEO-CLASSICISM (1750–1850) A return to Greek classical formality in art & architecture in a response to (and rejection of) Baroque and Rococo.[*Piranesi, Adam, Soane*]

ROMANTICISM (1780–1850) The championing of human emotion, and the inspiration of the natural world in reaction to industry and the Enlightenment. [*Turner, Blake, Delacroix, Constable*]

ARTS & CRAFTS (1850–1870) Anti-industrial revival of authentic decorative, and functional craft, for social reform. [*William Morris*]

IMPRESSIONISM (1860s–80s) The exploration of color & technique to capture the transience of light. [*Monet, Sisley, Pissaro, Renoir*]

POINTILLISM (1880s) Painting style using small dots of primary color which merge to form an image. [*Seurat, Signac, Cross*]

POST-IMPRESSIONISM (1880–1910) A move away from Impressionistic representation, towards a more abstract and emotional approach. [*Cézanne, Gauguin, van Gogh*]

ART NOUVEAU (1890–1915) Detailed decorative style, using both fluid curved lines, and strict geometry. [*Beardsley, Klimt, Tiffany*]

FAUVISM (1900–1908) The French 'movement' championing daring, bold, colorful & exuberant work. [*Matisse, Rouault, Dufy*]

EXPRESSIONISM (1900–40s) A style emphasizing the emotions and responses of the artist, rather than the realistic depiction of a subject. [*Kandinsky, Grosz, Modigliani*]

CUBISM (1900s–20s) Developed by *Picasso* and *Braque*, and influenced by Cézanne and tribal art, Cubism sought ways to see the essence of the subject by showing all of its fragmented facets simultaneously.

SOME NOTABLE BELGIANS

Jean Aerts	*cyclist*	Cornelius Jansen	*theologian*
Leo Baekeland	*Bakelite inventor*	Roland de Lassus	*composer*
Jules Bordet	*scientist*	René Magritte	*painter*
Thiery Boutsen	*racing driver*	Eddy Merckx	*cyclist*
Jacques Brel	*singer*	Christophe Plantin	*typographer*
Pieter Breughel	*painter*	Plastique Bertrand	*musician*
Ernest Claes	*writer*	Georges Rémi	*creator of TinTin*
Pierre Culliford	*'Smurfs' creator*	Peter Paul Rubens	*painter*
Paul Delvaux	*painter*	Adolphe Sax	*saxophone inventor*
Lamoral Egmont	*statesman*	Georges Simenon	*writer*
Audrey Hepburn	*actress*	Jean-Claude Van Damme	*actor*

NAVAJO CODE TALKERS

The Navajo code talkers participated in every assault conducted by the US Marines between 1942–5; their language code was never cracked. Phillip Johnston, the son of a missionary to the Navajos, was aware that obscure languages had been used as codes in previous wars. He convinced Major General Vogel to utilize the complex and unwritten Navajo language and, in 1942, twenty nine Navajo code talkers were recruited into the Marines. The value of the code talkers, for a generation kept a classified secret, cannot be underestimated. Major Howard Conner declared: 'Were it not for the Navajos, the Marines would never have taken Iwo Jima.' A lexicon of military and strategic terms was specially created to augment the Navajo language, a few of which are shown below:

STRATEGIC TERM	LITERAL TRANSLATION	NAVAJO WORD
Major	gold oak leaf	*che-chil-be-tah-ola*
Executive Officer	those in charge	*bih-da-hol-nehi*
Britain	between waters	*toh-ta*
Australia	rolled hat	*cha-yes-desi*
Russia	red army	*sila-gol-chi-ih*
Germany	iron hat	*besh-be-cha-he*
Dive bomber	chicken hawk	*gini*
Fighter plane	humming bird	*da-he-tih-hi*
Submarine	iron fish	*besh-lo*
August	big harvest	*be-neen-ta-tso*
December	crusted snow	*yas-nil-tes*

ZIP CODE

The term 'ZIP' is an acronym for the Zone Improvement Plan.

U AND NON-U

In 1954, Prof. Alan Ross published his essay 'Linguistic class-indicators in present-day English' in the renowned Finnish philological journal, *Neuphilologische Mitteilungen*. Here, Ross attempted to codify the spoken and written linguistic rules which demarcated upper-class language. His premise was that very subtle norms of phrasing, pronunciation, or vocabulary would instantly distinguish an upper-class ('U') speaker from the working or aspirational middle-classes ('non-U') speaker – as below:

NON-U	U	NON-U	U
to take a bath	to have a bath	perfume	scent
cycle	bicycle	note-paper	writing-paper
dinner	lunch	pardon?	what?
supper	dinner	preserve	jam
dress suit	dinner jacket	business/calling card	card
greens	vegetables	radio	wireless
horse-riding	riding	toilet	lavatory
jack (in cards)	knave	wealthy	rich
home	house	sweet	pudding
mirror	looking-glass	wire	telegram

1/299,792,458

Since 1983, the *meter* has been defined internationally as the length of the path traveled by light in a vacuum during 1/299,792,458th of a second. Importantly, a *second* is in turn defined as the duration of 9,192,631,770 periods of the radiation corresponding to the transition between the two hyperfine levels of the ground state of the caesium-133 atom.

MEASURING BRA SIZES

First, while wearing a bra, measure around the rib cage, directly under your bust. Add 5" to odd numbers, and 4" to even numbers. This is your band or bra size, e.g. 31"+5"=36" or 34"+4"=38". Then, measure the fullest part of the bust. The difference between the full bust measurement and the band or bra size gives the cup size as the following table indicates:

difference	*cup size*		
1"< bra size	AA	3" > bra size	D
= bra size	A	4" > bra size	DD
1" > bra size	B	5" > bra size	E
2" > bra size	C	6" > bra size	F
		7" > bra size	G

——— SCHEMATIC OF DANTE'S INFERNO ———

Some Inhabitants	*Region of Hell*	*Punishment*
Leopard, lion, she-wolf	FOREST	
Pope Celestine V	VESTIBULE	Pursued by insects
[Charon, the ferryman]	~ *River Acheron* ~	*'Upper Hell'*
Homer, Socrates, Plato	1 — LIMBO — 1	Desire without hope
[Minòs] Dido, Cleopatra	2 — THE LUSTFUL — 2	Battered by violent winds
[Cerberus] Ciacco	3 — THE GLUTTONOUS — 3	Besieged by foul weather
[Plutus]	4 — THE AVARICIOUS — 4	Perpetual violence
	THE ANGRY & SULLEN	Submerged in Styx
[Phlegyas, the boatman]	5 ~ *River Styx* ~ 5	*'Lower Hell', City of Dis*
Frederick II	6 — THE HERETICS — 6	Burned in tombs
[Minotaur]	7 — THE VIOLENT — 7	
[Centaurs]	~ *River Phlegethon* ~	
Alexander, Attila	*Violent against Others*	Drowned in hot blood
della Vigna, Lano Da Siena	*Suicides and Squanderers*	Enclosed in trees
Capaneus	*Violent against God or Nature*	Burned on hot sands
Brunetto Latini	*Unnatural Lust*	Forced perpetually to run
[Geryon]	8 — SIMPLE FRAUD — 8	*'Maleboge'*
Venedico Caccianemico	*Panderers & Seducers*	Whipped to walk endlessly
Alessio Interminei, Thais	*Flatterers*	Sunk in excrement
Pope Nicholas III	*Simoniacs*	Inverted and burned
Tiresias, Guido Bonatti	*Astrologers and Magicians*	Heads twisted round
[Malacoda &c.] Ciampolo	*Barrators*	Burned with pitch
Caiaphas, Annas	*Hypocrites*	Clad in weights
Vanni Fucci, Cacus	*Thieves*	Attacked by serpents
Ulysses, Diomed	*Fraudulent Counsellors*	Burned with flames
Bertram De Born	*Sowers of Discord*	Endlessly mutilated
Gianni Schicchi, Sinon	*Alchemists, Falsifiers*	Pain, filth, disease, attack
Nimrod, Antaeus, Ephialtes	THE GIANTS	Bound in chains
	~ *Frozen Lake of River Cocytus* ~	*'Cocytus'*
	9 — TREACHEROUS FRAUD — 9	
Napoleone Degli Alberti	*Traitors to Kin*	Up to shoulders in ice
Archbishop Ruggieri	*Traitors to Country*	Up to neck in ice
Branca D'Oria	*Traitors to Guests*	Immersed in ice
Judas, Brutus, Cassius	*Traitors to Benefactors & God*	Held in Lucifer's mouth

† LUCIFER †

---------------------- EXECUTIVE CLEMENCY ----------------------

The power of the President to exercise Executive Clemency is enshrined in Article II, Section 2, of the Constitution. Clemency can apply only to federal criminal offenses, and can take a number of forms including: pardon, commutation of sentence, remission of fine or restitution, and reprieve. The exercise of Executive Clemency has a long and controversial history, since it has been used as often for political gain as to right some judicial wrong. Perhaps the most famous pardon in American history was that granted by President Gerald Ford to ex-President Richard Nixon. In Proclamation 4311, September 8, 1974, Ford issued his pardon on the grounds that judicial action against Nixon would 'cause prolonged and divisive debate over the propriety of exposing to further punishment and degradation a man who has already paid the unprecedented penalty of relinquishing the highest elective office of the United States'.

---------------- HUSBANDS OF ELIZABETH TAYLOR ----------------

Elizabeth Taylor (1932–) has had eight marriages and seven husbands:

Nicky Hilton 1950–1	Richard Burton . . . 1964–74, 1975–6
Michael Wilding 1952–7	John Warner 1976–82
Michael Todd 1957–8	Larry Fortensky 1991–6
Eddie Fisher 1959–64	*[Husbands complete to January 2003]*

------------------------ WEATHER PROVERBS ------------------------

Red sky at night, shepherds'
delight, red sky in the morning,
shepherds' warning.

March winds and April showers
bring forth May flowers.

Clear moon, frost soon.

Halo around the sun or moon,
rain or snow is coming soon.

One swallow does not
a summer make.

Dew on the grass, rain shan't pass.

Rain before seven, fine by eleven.

Evening red and morning gray,
two sure signs of a perfect day.

The sudden storm lasts
not three hours.

The higher the clouds,
the better the weather.

Cold is the night when the
stars shine bright.

The farther the sight,
the nearer the rain.

APOTHECARIES' CONVERSIONS

WEIGHTS		MEASURES	
20 grains	1 scruple	20 minims	1 fl. scruple
3 scruples	1 drachm	3 fl. scruples	1 fl. drachm
8 drachms	1 ounce	8 fl. drachms	1 fl. ounce
12 ounces	1 pound	20 fl. ounces	1 pint

SUPPLIERS TO QUEEN ELIZABETH II

CHOCOLATE MANUFACTURERS	*Charbonnel et Walker*
GREENGROCER AND FLORIST	*Aboyne & Ballater Flowers*
BESOM BROOMS & PEA STICKS	*A. Nash*
POTTED SHRIMPS	*James Baxter & Son*
FRUIT JUICES & SOFT DRINKS	*Britvic Soft Drinks*
BISCUIT MANUFACTURERS	*William Crawford & Sons*
CANDLEMAKERS	*Price's Patent Candle Co.*
MOTOR LUBRICANTS	*Castrol*
BUTCHERS	*Cobb of Knightsbridge*
WINE MERCHANTS	*Corney & Barrow*
SCOTCH WHISKY DISTILLERS	*William Sanderson & Son*
PORK SAUSAGES	*Fairfax Meadow Farm*
CHEESEMAKERS	*Howgate Dairy Foods*
GROCERS & PROVISIONS	*Fortnum & Mason*
STATIONERS	*Frank Smythson*
COACH PAINTS	*Akzo Nobel C.T. Coatings*
PICTURE FRAMERS	*Petersfield Book Shop*
PIANOFORTE MANUFACTURERS	*John Broadwood & Sons*
BAGPIPE MAKERS	*R G Hardie & Co*
RESTORER OF FINE-ART OBJECTS	*Plowden & Smith*
FINE-ART DEALERS	*Hazlitt Gooden & Fox*
ANGOSTURA BITTERS	*Angostura Ltd*
ROSES	*James Cocker & Sons*
PHILATELISTS	*Stanley Gibbons*
GUNSMITHS	*Gallyon & Sons*
BOOKSELLERS	*Alden & Blackwell*
BRASS FINISHERS & SPRING MAKERS	*Cope & Timmins*
CHRISTMAS CRACKERS	*Tom Smith Group*

SEVEN SEAS

Antarctic · Arctic · North Atlantic · South Atlantic
Indian Ocean · North Pacific · South Pacific

PHILATELIC GLOSSARY

Below are a few of the many terms used by stamp dealers and collectors.

ALBINO a stamp rendered colorless by a printing error.

PHOSPHOR marks or bands of a fluorescent substance to be read by automatic sorting machines.

BISECT a stamp legitimately cut in half to pay postage at half the rate.

CACHET a handstamp used to commemorate a special edition.

SE-TENANT two or more stamps issued joined together but with different values or designs, often used to form composite designs.

TÊTE-BÊCHE a pair of adjoined stamps, one upside-down.

DRY PRINT a stamp with a weak or pale image due to insufficient ink.

ERROR stamps erroneously issued with incorrect designs.

PLATE NUMBER an identifying mark in the margin of a sheet.

FISCAL STAMPS a stamp issued for the collection of tax.

SURCHARGE an overprint which changes the face value of a stamp.

CREASY'S DECISIVE BATTLES

In his 1851 book, *The Fifteen Decisive Battles of the World*, Professor Sir Edward Shepherd Creasy (1812–78) gave his analysis of the moments of conflict which he claimed forever changed the course of world history.

Date	Battle	Decisive Action according to Creasy
BC 490	Marathon	*Greeks under Militades defeated the Persians*
413	Syracuse	*Peloponnesian War limiting Greek expansion*
331	Arbela	*Alexander overthrew Darius*
207	Metaurus	*Romans defeated Hasdrubal*
AD 9	Teutoberger Wald	*Germanic forces defeated the Romans*
451	Châlons	*Attila's defeat by Aetius*
732	Tours	*Charles Martel overthrew the Saracens*
1066	Hastings	*Norman Conquest of England*
1429	Orléans	*Joan of Arc secured French independence*
1588	Spanish Armada	*England's defeat of the Spanish*
1704	Blenheim	*Marlborough's defeat of Tallard*
1709	Pultowa	*Russia's defeat of Sweden*
1777	Saratoga	*Gates defeated Burgoyne*
1792	Valmy	*Revolutionists' defeat of allies under Brunswick*
1815	Waterloo	*Wellington's defeat of Napoleon*

SEABREEZE

2 vodka · 3 cranberry juice · 2 grapefruit juice · lime peel

KENTUCKY DERBY WINNERS

Year	*Horse*	*Time*	*Jockey*	*Lengths*	*Track*
'80	Genuine Risk	2:02	J. Vasquez	1	F
'81	Pleasant Colony	2:02	J. Velasquez	¾	F
'82	Gato Del Sol	2:02	E. Delahoussaye	2½	F
'83	Sunny's Halo	2:02	E. Delahoussaye	2	F
'84	Swale	2:02	L. Pincay, Jr.	3¼	F
'85	Spend a Buck	2:00	A. Cordero, Jr.	5¾	F
'86	Ferdinand	2:02	W. Shoemaker	2¼	F
'87	Alysheba	2:03	C. McCarron	¾	F
'88	Winning Colors	2:02	G. Stevens	neck	F
'89	Sunday Silence	2:05	P. Valenzuela	2½	M
'90	Unbridled	2:02	C. Perret	3½	G
'91	Strike the Gold	2:03	C. Antleya	1¾	F
'92	Lil E. Tee	2:03	P. Day	1	F
'93	Sea Hero	2:02	J. Bailey	2½	F
'94	Go for Gin	2:03	C. McCarron	2	M
'95	Thunder Gulch	2:01	G. Stevens	2¼	F
'96	Grindstone	2:01	J. Bailey	nose	F
'97	Silver Charm	2:02	G. Stevens	head	F
'98	Real Quiet	2:02	K. Desormeaux	½	F
'99	Charismatic	2:03	C. Antley	neck	F
'00	Fusaichi Pegasus	2:01	K. Desormeaux	1½	F
'01	Monarchos	1:59	Jorge Chavez	4¾	F
'02	War Emblem	2:01	Victor Espinoza	4	F

Times rounded up to the second · Track Condition: Fast · Muddy · Good

THE VOICES OF MEL BLANC

The most famous voice-actor in film history, Mel Blanc (1908–89) got his first break in 1937 working with Tex Avery on *Picador Porky.* Over the years Blanc voiced dozens of characters, some of which are shown below:

Woody Woodpecker	Porky the Pig	Marvin the Martian
Daffy Duck	Pancho	The Road Runner
Foghorn Leghorn	Sad Sack	Barney Rubble
Sylvester Pussycat	Speedy Gonzales	Dino
Bugs Bunny	Pepe LePew	The Tasmanian Devil

CHINESE ZODIAC YEARS

RAT · 1912 · 1924 · 1936 · 1948 · 1960 · 1972 · 1984 · 1996 · 2008

OX · 1913 · 1925 · 1937 · 1949 · 1961 · 1973 · 1985 · 1997 · 2009

TIGER · 1914 · 1926 · 1938 · 1950 · 1962 · 1974 · 1986 · 1998 · 2010

RABBIT · 1915 · 1927 · 1939 · 1951 · 1963 · 1975 · 1987 · 1999 · 2011

DRAGON · 1916 · 1928 · 1940 · 1952 · 1964 · 1976 · 1988 · 2000 · 2012

SNAKE · 1917 · 1929 · 1941 · 1953 · 1965 · 1977 · 1989 · 2001 · 2013

HORSE · 1918 · 1930 · 1942 · 1954 · 1966 · 1978 · 1990 · 2002 · 2014

RAM · 1919 · 1931 · 1943 · 1955 · 1967 · 1979 · 1991 · 2003 · 2015

MONKEY · 1920 · 1932 · 1944 · 1956 · 1968 · 1980 · 1992 · 2004 · 2016

ROOSTER · 1921 · 1933 · 1945 · 1957 · 1969 · 1981 · 1993 · 2005 · 2017

DOG · 1922 · 1934 · 1946 · 1958 · 1970 · 1982 · 1994 · 2006 · 2018

BOAR/PIG · 1923 · 1935 · 1947 · 1959 · 1971 · 1983 · 1995 · 2007 · 2019

SPECIFICATIONS OF THE ARK

Made from	gopherwood	Decks	3
Length	300 cubits	Number of humans	8
Breadth	50 cubits	Rain duration	40 days & nights
Height	30 cubits	Flood prevailed for	150 days
Windows	1	Noah lived to	950 years

CHESS TERMS

BAD BISHOP A bishop unable to move freely because of friendly pawns, themselves unable to move.

BASE OF PAWN CHAIN the last and weakest pawn in a diagonal chain.

BURIED PIECE one hemmed in by friendly pieces.

CASTLE moving the king two squares either right or left, and placing the rook on the square beside the king closest to the center.

CENTER the four center squares.

DEVELOPMENT bringing pieces into play.

DIAGONAL lines moved by bishops and queens from North East to South West, or from North West to South East.

DISCOVERED CHECK check given by one piece as the result of the moving away of another piece that was masking it.

DOUBLED PAWNS two pawns of the same color on the same file.

EN PASSANT where a pawn on the 5th rank captures an opponent's pawn on an adjacent file, which has just moved 2 squares forward on its first move.

EN PRISE an unprotected piece vulnerable to capture.

FILE a vertical row of squares.

J'ADOUBE or I ADJUST said to warn that a piece is merely being adjusted and not actually played.

PERPETUAL CHECK an endless attack on a king which will not lead to checkmate. Often this position results in a draw.

PIN a piece which masks another from attack.

PROMOTION a pawn which reaches the final rank can be 'promoted' to a queen, rook, bishop, or knight (usually a queen – hence the alternate term often employed: QUEENING).

RANK a horizontal row of squares.

SACRIFICE (or SAC) the deliberate loss of a piece for tactical gain.

SANS VOIR playing blindfolded.

SKEWER when a piece is forced to move exposing another piece to capture.

STALEMATE a drawn game where no legal move is playable.

WAITING MOVE a benign move designed to change the turn.

ZUGZWANG a position whereby any move is disadvantageous.

ZWISCHENZUG an unexpected move played within a sequence.

——— SOME PHILOSOPHICAL QUOTATIONS ———

FRIEDRICH NIETZSCHE · God is dead: but considering the state the species of Man is in, there will perhaps be caves, for ages yet, in which his shadow will be shown.

SIGMUND FREUD · Anatomy is destiny.

MICHAEL OAKESHOTT · Anyone who has had a glimpse of the range and subtlety of the thought of Plato or of Hegel will long ago have despaired of becoming a philosopher.

THOMAS HOBBES · [*on the state of nature*] No arts; no letters; no society; and which is worst of all, continual fear and danger of violent death; and the life of man, solitary, poor, nasty, brutish and short.

RENÉ DESCARTES · *Cogito ergo sum* (I think therefore I am).

CICERO · The good of the people is the chief law.

ADAM SMITH · Science is the great antidote to the poison of enthusiasm and superstition.

JEREMY BENTHAM · The greatest happiness of the greatest number is the foundation of morals and legislation.

ARISTOTLE · Poetry is more philosophical and more serious than history, for its statements are in the nature of universals, whereas those of history are singulars.

IMMANUEL KANT · Out of the crooked tree of humanity no straight thing can ever be made.

BENEDICT SPINOZA · All noble things are as difficult as they are rare.

BERTRAND RUSSELL · If one man offers you democracy and another offers you a bag of grain, at what stage of starvation will you prefer the grain to the vote?

BLAISE PASCAL · I lay it down as a fact that if all men knew what others say of them, there would not be four friends in the world.

DIONYSIUS OF HALICARNASSUS History is philosophy derived from examples.

ÉMILE DURKHEIM · There is no society known where a more or less developed criminality is not found under different forms.

WILLIAM OF OCCAM · No more things should be presumed to exist than are absolutely necessary.

JEAN-PAUL SARTRE · Everything is gratuitous, this garden, this city and myself. When you suddenly realize it, it makes you feel sick and everything begins to drift ... that's nausea.

HENRY DAVID THOREAU · Some circumstantial evidence is very strong, as when you find a trout in the milk.

——— PHILOSOPHICAL QUOTATIONS cont. ———

ERICH FROMM · There is perhaps no phenomenon which contains so much destructive feeling as 'moral indignation', which permits envy or hate to be acted out under the guise of virtue.

FRIEDRICH ENGELS · The State is not 'abolished', it withers away.

GEORGE BERKELEY · Truth is the cry of all, but the game of few.

THEODORE ADORNO · The total effect of the culture industry is one of anti-enlightenment ... the progressive technical domination of nature, becomes mass deception and is turned into a means for fettering consciousness.

GEORG HEGEL · When philosophy paints its gray on gray, then has a shape of life grown old. By philosophy's gray on gray it cannot be rejuvenated but only understood. The owl of Minerva spreads its wings only with the falling of the dusk.

LUDWIG WITTGENSTEIN · The face is the soul of the body.

ISAIAH BERLIN · The fundamental sense of freedom is freedom from chains, from imprisonment, from enslavement by others. The rest is extension of this sense, or else metaphor.

GEORGE BERNARD SHAW · There is only one religion, though there are a hundred versions of it.

SOCRATES · The unexamined life is not worth living.

THOMAS AQUINAS · Man has free choice, or otherwise counsels, exhortations, commands, prohibitions, rewards and punishments would be in vain.

GOTTFRIED LEIBNIZ · There are two kinds of truths: those of reasoning and those of fact. The truths of reasoning are necessary and their opposite is impossible; the truths of fact are contingent and their opposites are possible.

KARL POPPER · In so far as a scientific statement speaks about reality, it must be falsifiable: and in so far as it is not falsifiable, it does not speak about reality.

FRANCIS BACON · If a man will begin with certainties, he shall end in doubts; but if he will be content to begin with doubts, he shall end in certainties.

J.S. MILL · War is an ugly thing, but not the ugliest of things: the decayed and degraded state of moral and patriotic feeling which thinks nothing worth a war, is worse.

MARCUS AURELIUS · Every instant of time is a pinprick of eternity. All things are petty, easily changed, vanishing away.

LEO TOLSTOY· Friedrich Nietzsche was stupid and abnormal.

POTENTIAL OF HYDROGEN

pH *(Potential of Hydrogen)* is a measure of acidity and alkalinity. The pH is defined as the negative logarithm of the hydrogen-ion concentration: or $pH = \log_{10} 1/[H^+]$. The pH of pure water is 7 or neutral $(\log_{10} 1/[10^{-7}])$; acids have a pH<7; and alkalies have a pH>7. The scale is logarithmic, so pH1 is 10x more acidic than pH2. Below are some approximate values:

0.1	hydrochloric acid	6.4	saliva
0.3	sulphuric acid	6.8	milk
1.0	stomach acid	7.0	distilled water
2.3	lemon juice	7.4	blood
2.8	vinegar	8.0	seawater
5.0	black coffee	9.0	baking soda
5.2	acid rain	10.5	milk of magnesia
5.5	white bread	11.0	domestic bleach
5.7	rainwater	14.0	caustic soda

COOKING TEMPERATURES

Description	°C	°F	Gas Mark	Aga[†]
very slow	110	225	¼	very cool
	120	250	½	
	140	275	1	
slow	150	300	2	cool
	160–70	325	3	warm
moderate	180	350	4	
	190	375	5	medium
moderate hot	200	400	6	medium high
	220	425	7	
hot	230	450	8	high
very hot	240–60	475	9	very high

[†] 'Aga' is an acronym derived from the maker: *Svenska [A]ktienbolaget [G]as[a]kumulator Co.*

THE HIERARCHY OF FALCONRY

In her idiosyncratic 1486 *Boke of St Albans*, Dame Julia Berners presents a hierarchy of hawks and the social ranks with which they are appropriate:

Gerfalcon	King	Merlin	Lady
Peregrine Falcon	Earl	Tercel	Poorman
Bastard Hawk	Baron	Sparrowhawk	Priest
Lanner & Lanneret	Squire	Kestrel	Servant or Knave

COMPASS POINTS

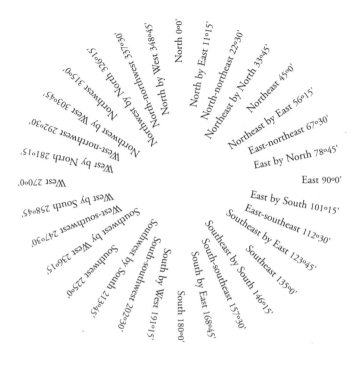

North 0°0'
North by East 11°15'
North-northeast 22°30'
Northeast by North 33°45'
Northeast 45°0'
Northeast by East 56°15'
East-northeast 67°30'
East by North 78°45'
East 90°0'
East by South 101°15'
East-southeast 112°30'
Southeast by East 123°45'
Southeast 135°0'
Southeast by South 146°15'
South-southeast 157°30'
South by East 168°45'
South 180°0'
South by West 191°15'
South-southwest 202°30'
Southwest by South 213°45'
Southwest 225°0'
Southwest by West 236°15'
West-southwest 247°30'
West by South 258°45'
West 270°0'
West by North 281°15'
West-northwest 292°30'
Northwest by West 303°45'
Northwest 315°0'
Northwest by North 326°15'
North-northwest 337°30'
North by West 348°45'

FREUD & THE MIND

ID (derived from the Latin word for 'It') is the elemental, unconscious and uncivilized mind. It is the center of basic, primitive instincts and urges, and is geared towards selfishness and survival. The Id is best personified by the urges and behavior of the new-born baby.

EGO (derived from the Latin for 'I') is the conscious and preconscious mind which civilizes the Id, and recognizes the existence of a wider world. The Ego represses inappropriate urges of the Id, and conflict between the Ego and the Id is the cause of neuroses.

SUPEREGO is the highest state of mind to which we have evolved. It is our conscience, regulating our thoughts and actions, checking the demands of the Id and the Ego. The Superego reacts and responds to the sophisticated rules and norms of society.

SOME LEFT-HANDERS

Lewis Carroll	Tiberius	Prince Charles	Paul Klee
Gary Sobers	George VI	Paul McCartney	Bob Dylan
Albert Einstein	Nietzsche	M.C. Escher	Bill Clinton
Bill Gates	Fidel Castro	Queen Victoria	H.G. Wells
Cole Porter	Pelé	Phil Collins	Elizabeth II

SNEEZING

If you sneeze on Monday, you sneeze for danger;
Sneeze on Tuesday, kiss a stranger;
Sneeze on Wednesday, sneeze for a letter;
Sneeze on Thursday, something better;
Sneeze on Friday, sneeze for sorrow;
Sneeze on Saturday, see your sweetheart tomorrow.

WINDS

There are many systems of nomenclature for the naming of winds; they vary by location, language, and tradition. One of the systems which is often seen around the edges of old maps is based on the following names:

Tramontana	Northerly	Ostro	Southerly
Greco	North-easterly	Libeccio	South-westerly
Levante	Easterly	Ponente	Westerly
Sirocco	South-easterly	Maestro	North-westerly

ADULT DENTITION

After the age of six or so, the 'milk-teeth' are replaced by 32 adult teeth: 8 incisors · 4 canines · 8 pre-molars · 12 molars (4 being 'wisdom teeth')

TEMPERATURE CONVERSION

To convert º Celsius to º Fahrenheit........ multiply by 1.8 and add 32
To convert º Fahrenheit to º Celsius....... subtract 32 and divide by 1.8

Rule-of-Thumb Approximate Reversible Temperatures
16 º Centigrade = 61 º Fahrenheit
28 º Centigrade = 82 º Fahrenheit

INTERNATIONAL WASHING SYMBOLS

WASHING							
	Maximum Temperature	Hand Wash	*Bars under the washing symbol can have different meanings. Always check.*	Cotton / Normal	Synthetics / Permapress	Wool / Gentle	Do not Wash

BLEACHING					OTHER		
	Chlorine bleach	Chlorine bleach	Non-chlorine bleach	Do not Bleach		No Heat or Air	Do not wring

IRONING							
	Iron on low	Iron on medium	Iron on high	Maximum temperature	Steam	No steam	Do not Iron

DRYING							
	Tumble dry low	Tumble dry medium	Tumble dry high	Drip-dry	Dry flat	Line-dry	Do not tumble dry

DRY CLEANING						
	Dry clean	Any solvent	Not trichloro-ethylene	Petroleum solvent	*Additional markings give specialist information to professional dry-cleaners.*	Do not dry clean

Symbols and their meaning can vary around the world. Seek advice before cleaning.

DRIVING ON THE LEFT

Anguilla · Antigua · Australia · Bahamas · Bangladesh · Barbados
Bermuda · Bhutan · Botswana · British Virgin Islands · Brunei
Cayman Islands · Channel Islands · Ciskei · Cook Islands · Cyprus
Dominica · Falkland Islands · Fiji Islands · Grenada · Guyana
Hong Kong · India · Indonesia · Republic of Ireland · Jamaica · Japan
Kenya · Kiribati · Lesotho · Macau · Malawi · Malaysia · Malta
Mauritius · Montserrat · Mozambique · Namibia · Nepal · New Zealand
Niue · Norfolk Islands · Pakistan · Papua New Guinea · Seychelles
Sikkim · Singapore · Solomon Islds · Somalia · South Africa · Sri Lanka
St Helena · St Kitts & Nevis · St Lucia · St Vincent · Surinam
Swaziland · Tanzania · Thailand · Tonga · Trinidad & Tobago · Tuvalu
Uganda · UK[†] · US Virgin Islands · Venda · Zambia · Zimbabwe

[†] *Except in Savoy Court, off Strand in London, where traffic must drive on the right.*

State	Capital	Admission order	Admission date	Abbreviation	max speed limit mph	Has death penalty	Original Colony	No. of Miss Americas	Foreign borders	State Bird	Inhabitants called
Alabama	Montgomery	22	12-14-1819	AL	70	†		2		Yellowhammer	Alabam(i)an
Alaska	Juneau	49	01-03-1959	AK	65				‡	Willow Ptarmigan	Alaskan
Arizona	Phoenix	48	02-14-1912	AZ	75	†		2	‡	Cactus Wren	Arizon(i)an
Arkansas	Little Rock	25	06-15-1836	AR	70	†		2		Mockingbird	Arkansan
California	Sacramento	31	09-09-1850	CA	70	†		6	‡	California Valley Quail	Californian
Colorado	Denver	38	08-01-1876	CO	75	†		3		Lark Bunting	Colorad(o)an
Connecticut	Hartford	5	01-09-1788	CT	65		§	1		Robin	Connecticuter
Delaware	Dover	1	12-07-1787	DE	65		§			Blue Hen Chicken	Delawarean
Florida	Tallahassee	27	03-03-1845	FL	70	†		1		Mockingbird	Florid(i)an
Georgia	Atlanta	4	01-02-1788	GA	70		§	1		Brown Thrasher	Georgian
Hawaii	Honolulu	50	08-21-1959	HI	60			2		Nene	Hawaiian
Idaho	Boise	43	07-03-1890	ID	75	†			‡	Mountain Bluebird	Idahoan
Illinois	Springfield	21	12-03-1818	IL	65	†		4		Cardinal	Illinoisan
Indiana	Indianapolis	19	12-11-1816	IN	65	†				Cardinal	Indian(i)an
Iowa	Des Moines	29	12-28-1846	IA	65					Eastern Goldfinch	Iowan
Kansas	Topeka	34	01-29-1861	KS	70	†		3		Western Meadowlark	Kansan
Kentucky	Frankfort	15	06-01-1792	KY	65	†		1		Cardinal	Kentuckian
Louisiana	Baton Rouge	18	04-30-1812	LA	70	†				Eastern Brown Pelican	Louisian(i)an
Maine	Augusta	23	03-15-1820	ME	65				‡	Chickadee	Mainer
Maryland	Annapolis	7	04-28-1788	MD	65	†	§			Baltimore Oriole	Marylander
Massachusetts	Boston	6	02-06-1788	MA	65		§			Chickadee	Bay Stater

State	Capital	Admission order	Admission date	Abbreviation	max. speed limit mph	Has death penalty	Original Colony	No. of Miss Americas	Foreign borders	State Bird	Inhabitants called
Michigan	Lansing	26	01-26-1837	MI	70			4	‡	Robin	Michigander
Minnesota	St. Paul	32	05-11-1858	MN	70			3	‡	Common Loon	Minnesotan
Mississippi	Jackson	20	12-10-1817	MS	70	†		4		Mockingbird	Mississippian
Missouri	Jefferson City	24	08-10-1821	MO	70	†		1		Bluebird	Missourian
Montana	Helena	41	11-08-1889	MT	75	†			‡	Western Meadowlark	Montanan
Nebraska	Lincoln	37	03-01-1867	NE	75	†				Western Meadowlark	Nebraskan
Nevada	Carson City	36	10-31-1864	NV	75	†				Mountain Bluebird	Nevad(i)an
New Hampshire	Concord	9	06-21-1788	NH	65	†	$		‡	Purple Finch	New Hampshirite
New Jersey	Trenton	3	12-18-1787	NJ	65	†	$	2		Eastern Goldfinch	New Jerseyite (-ian)
New Mexico	Santa Fe	47	01-06-1912	NM	75	†			‡	Roadrunner	New Mexican
New York	Albany	11	07-26-1788	NY	65	†	$	3	‡	Bluebird	New Yorker
North Carolina	Raleigh	12	11-21-1789	NC	70	†	$	1		Cardinal	North Carolinian
North Dakota	Bismarck	39	11-02-1889	ND	70				‡	Western Meadowlark	North Dakotan
Ohio	Columbus	17	03-01-1803	OH	65	†		6		Cardinal	Ohioan
Oklahoma	Oklahoma City	46	11-16-1907	OK	75	†		4		Scissor-tailed Flycatcher	Oklahoman
Oregon	Salem	33	02-14-1859	OR	65	†		1		Western Meadowlark	Oregonian
Pennsylvania	Harrisburg	2	12-12-1787	PA	65	†	$	5		Ruffed Grouse	Pennsylvanian
Rhode Island	Providence	13	05-29-1790	RI	65		$			Rhode Island Red	Rhode Islander
South Carolina	Columbia	8	05-23-1788	SC	70	†	$	2		Great Carolina Wren	South Carolinian
South Dakota	Pierre	40	11-02-1889	SD	75	†				Ring-necked Pheasant	South Dakotan
Tennessee	Nashville	16	06-01-1796	TN	70	†		2		Mockingbird	Tennesse(e)an

—— STATES cont. ——

State	Capital	Admission order	Admission date	Abbreviation	max speed limit	Has death penalty	Original Colony	Miss Americas	Foreign borders	State Bird	Inhabitants called
Texas	Austin	28	12-29-1845	TX	70	†		3	‡	Mockingbird	Texan
Utah	Salt Lake City	45	01-04-1896	UT	75	†		2		California Seagull	Utah(a)n
Vermont	Montpelier	14	03-04-1791	VT	65				‡	Hermit Thrush	Vermonter
Virginia	Richmond	10	06-25-1788	VA	65	†	§	2		Cardinal	Virginian
Washington	Olympia	42	11-11-1889	WA	70	†				Willow Goldfinch	Washingtonian
West Virginia	Charleston	35	06-20-1863	WV	70					Cardinal	Virginian
Wisconsin	Madison	30	05-29-1848	WI	65			1		Robin	Wisconsinite
Wyoming	Cheyenne	44	07-10-1890	WY	75	†				Western Meadowlark	Wyomingite

— SOME 10-CODES —

10-1 / 10-2	Signal weak / good
10-3	Stop Transmitting
10-4	Affirmative (OK)
10-5	Relay (to)
10-6	Busy
10-7 / 10-8	Out of / in service
10-9	Say Again
10-10	Negative
10-11	On Duty
10-12	Stand By (wait)
10-14	Message / Information
10-15	Message Delivered
10-16	Reply to Message
10-17	Enroute
10-18	Urgent
10-19	(In) Contact
10-20	Location
10-21	Call *x* by Phone
10-22	Disregard
10-23	Arrived at Scene
10-24	Assignment Completed
10-25	Report to (meet)
10-26	Estimated Arrival Time
10-27	License Information
10-30	Danger/Caution
10-31	Pick Up
10-32	Units Needed
10-33	Help Me Quick
10-34	Time

—PHONETIC DIGITS—

0	Nadazero	*nah-dah-zer-roh*
1	Unaone	*oo-nah-wun*
2	Bissotwo	*bee-soh-too*
3	Terrathree	*tey-rah-tree*
4	Kartefour	*kar-tay-fower*
5	Pantafive	*pan-tah-five*
6	Soxisix	*sok-see-six*
7	Setteseven	*say-tay-seven*
8	Oktoeight	*ok-tow-ait*
9	Novenine	*no-vey-nine*

ENGLISH TO AMERICAN ENGLISH

'England and America are two countries divided by a common language'
– George Bernard Shaw

English	American
Athlete	jock
Aubergine	eggplant
Pushchair	stroller
Banger	sausage / old car
Bonnet (of car)	hood
Boot (of car)	trunk
Bumbag	fanny pack
Central reservation	median strip
Chicory	endive
Dummy	pacifier
Economy (airfare)	coach
Ex-directory (phone)	unlisted
Faggot	meatball
Fringe (hair)	bangs
Guillotine	paper cutter
Headmaster	principal
Hundreds & thousands	sprinkles
Jumper	sweater
Kipper	smoked herring
Mileometer	odometer
Muesli	granola
Number plate	license plate
Paraffin	kerosene
Pelican crossing	cross-walk
Plait (hair)	braid
Plonk	(cheap) wine
Postcode	zip code
Potato crisps	chips
Pub	bar
Punter	customer
Quay	wharf/pier
Queue	line
Secondary school	high school
Skip (for rubbish)	dumpster
Skirting board	baseboard
Skive	goof off
Sleeping policeman	speed bump
Smart	well-dressed
Snog (kiss)	make out with
Solicitor	attorney/lawyer
Straight (drink)	neat
Tap	faucet
Tarmac	blacktop
Tights	pantyhose
Treacle	molasses
Turn-ups (trousers)	cuffs (pants)
Vest	undershirt
Waistcoat	vest
Washing up	doing the dishes
Wellingtons	gumboots
Zebra crossing	pedestrian crossing

English say	Americans hear & say	English hear
trousers	pants	underwear
condom	rubber	eraser
braces	suspenders	garter-belt

A NOTE ON SCHOOL NOMENCLATURE

In Britain, both 'public' and 'private' schools are fee-paying, selective schools equivalent to the American private school. However, many in Britain recognize a subtle distinction between the two terms: public schools are usually considered to be the older and grander educational establishments (Eton, Harrow, Winchester, &c.), and are more likely to be boarding schools. The equivalent to the American public school is the British 'state' school – funded by the government and available to all.

SPECIFICATIONS OF THE EARTH

Equatorial radius ..... 6378.1 km	Surface gravity .... 980 cm/s^2
Polar radius .... 6356.8 km	Escape velocity .... 11.18 km/s
Volume ...... 259,875,300,000m^3	Planet Year .... 365.256 days
Mass .... 5.974 x 10^{27}g	Core temperature ..... 4500°C (est)
Age .... *c*.4,500,000,000 years	Water:land ratio ... 71%:29% (est)

FAMOUS LAST WORDS

RUDOLPH VALENTINO
Don't pull down the blinds!
I feel fine.
I want the sunlight to greet me.

EDVARD GRIEG
Well, if it must be so.

ARNOLD BENNETT
Everything has gone wrong, my girl.

JANE AUSTEN
[is there anything you require?]
Nothing but death.

DYLAN THOMAS
I've had eighteen straight whiskies,
I think that's a record.

BENJAMIN DISRAELI
I am not afraid to die.

GUSTAV MAHLER
Mozart!

CHARLES FOSTER KANE
Rosebud.

OSCAR WILDE
Either that wallpaper goes, or I do.

NOËL COWARD
Good night, my darlings, I'll see
you in the morning.

BLAISE PASCAL
May God never abandon me.

J.M. TURNER
The sun is God.

IMMANUEL KANT
It is enough.

WINSTON CHURCHILL
Oh, I am so bored with it all.

JAMES JOYCE
Does nobody understand?

THE CHATHAM HOUSE RULE

In order to encourage free and open debate on sensitive political issues, the Royal Institute of International Affairs, in 1927, devised the Chatham House Rule. Named after the Institute's London HQ, the Rule is a morally binding convention which allows all or part of a meeting to be held 'off the record'. Information gleaned under the Chatham House Rule may be reported, but the identity or affiliations of speakers must not be disclosed.

MORSE CODE

A	· —	A	M	— —	M	Y	— · — —	Y
B	— · · ·	B	N	— ·	N	Z	— — · ·	Z
C	— · — ·	C	O	— — —	O	0	— — — — —	0
D	— · ·	D	P	· — — ·	P	1	· — — — —	1
E	·	E	Q	— — · —	Q	2	· · — — —	2
F	· · — ·	F	R	· — ·	R	3	· · · — —	3
G	— — ·	G	S	· · ·	S	4	· · · · —	4
H	· · · ·	H	T	—	T	5	· · · · ·	5
I	· ·	I	U	· · —	U	6	— · · · ·	6
J	· — — —	J	V	· · · —	V	7	— — · · ·	7
K	— · —	K	W	· — —	W	8	— — — · ·	8
L	· — · ·	L	X	— · · —	X	9	— — — — ·	9

OFT CONFUSED WORDS

The CAPITOL building . . . . is situated in the CAPITAL city

The STATUE had such STATURE . . . . . . there was a STATUTE to protect it

Members of the COUNCIL . . . . . . mocked the lawyers for their COUNSEL

It is my guiding TENET . . . . to overcharge my TENANTS

Each business was a DISCRETE entity . . . . so we had to be DISCREET

A judge should be DISINTERESTED . . . . but never UNINTERESTED

The arrival of the EMINENT scientist . . . . . was thought to be IMMINENT

I tried to AFFECT the jury's decision . . . . the EFFECT of which was a fine

They FLAUNTED the fact . . . . that they FLOUTED the law

I was asked to FORWARD . . . . the new FOREWORD I had written

One should be WARY . . . . of driving when WEARY

Due to the RAIN throughout her REIGN . . . . . the Queen grips her REINS

After FLOUNDERING about . . . . he FOUNDERED beneath the waves

I took a PEEK at the mountain PEAK . . . which had PIQUED my curiosity

The school PRINCIPAL . . . . is a woman of few PRINCIPLES

The vehicle delivering STATIONERY . . . . was STATIONARY in traffic

The COMPLIMENTARY wine . . . . COMPLEMENTED the fish perfectly

I will ACCEPT all gifts . . . . EXCEPT those that are cheap

The police could not ELICIT a confession . . . . about his ILLICIT activities

The STRAIT of Hormuz . . . . is far from STRAIGHT

There was an ORDINANCE . . . . against firing any ORDNANCE

He was TAUGHT not to TAUNT . . . . the woman for her TAUT grip

Poor weather meant the GUERRILLAS shot . . . . the GORILLAS in the mist

This FOWL . . . . tastes FOUL

His company was INTOLERABLE . . . . because he was so INTOLERANT

Hospital PATIENTS . . . . need to have PATIENCE

Building SITES are splendid SIGHTS . . . . . . so we CITE them in the guide

——— ROUGH CLOTHING CONVERSIONS ———

Men's Shoes						
British	6	7	8	9	10	11
American	7½	8½	9½	10½	11½	12½
European	39½	40½	41½	42½	43½	44½
Women's Shoes						
British	3	4	5	6	7	8
American	4½	5½	6½	7½	8½	9½
European	35	36	37	38	39	40
Women's Clothes						
British	10	12	14	16	18	20
American	8	10	12	14	16	18
French	40	42	44	46	48	50
Italian	44	46	48	50	52	54
German	36	38	40	42	44	46
Men's Suits						
British	34	36	38	40	42	44
American	34	36	38	40	42	44
European	44	46	48	50	52	54
Men's Shirts						
British	14	14½	15	15½	16	16½	17
American	14	14½	15	15½	16	16½	17
European	36	37	38	39	40	41	42
Men's Socks						
British	9½	10	10½	11	11½	12	12½
American	9½	10	10½	11	11½	12	12½
European	38–9	39–40	40–1	41–2	42–3	43–4	44–5

——— POLO CHUKKAS ———

The game of Polo is divided into *chukkas* of seven and a half minutes. At the end of each *chukka* a bell is rung, and the play is extended for thirty seconds unless the ball goes out of play, or the umpire calls a foul. [The last *chukka* of a match stops after seven minutes with no additional time added.] Between each *chukka* there is a three-minute interval – extended to five minutes at half-time. A full match lasts for six *chukkas*, but sometimes four or eight are played by mutual agreement. If, at the end of the final *chukka*, the scores are tied, then an interval of five minutes is called, the distance between the goals is widened from eight to sixteen yards, and additional *chukkas* are played until the deciding goal is scored.

[*The* Oxford English Dictionary *gives the etymology of* chukka *as derived from the Hindustani* chakar *and the Sanskrit* cakra *meaning circle or wheel.*]

COMMONPLACE FRENCH
---

agent provocateur...............................one who incites another
amour-propre....................self-esteem, self-love; sometimes vanity
ancien régime.........the old regime; the regime before the present state
au fond..fundamentally
beau geste..a gesture of magnanimity
belle époque..................a golden age; in France, that preceding WWI
chacun à son goût...................................to each his own taste
comme il faut...........................correct; appropriate and fitting
de rigueur....................absolutely required (by social convention)
éminence grise..............................the power behind the throne
faute de mieux......................for the lack of any better alternative
fin de siècle........the end of the (nineteenth) century; decadent, louche
haut monde..fashionable society
idée fixe...an obsession
lèse-majesté..............................an offence against the Sovereign
noblesse oblige.............the obligations imposed by rank and privilege
raison d'être..the reason for existence
touché..................acknowledgement of a point scored in argument
trompe l'oeil........................painting style which deceives the eye

---
LINNAEAN ORDER OF CLASSIFICATION

KINGDOM
subkingdom
PHYLUM
subphylum
superclass
CLASS
subclass
infraclass
cohort
superorder
ORDER
suborder
superfamily
FAMILY
subfamily
tribe
GENUS
subgenus
SPECIES
subspecies

USEFUL WORDS FOR WORD GAMES

aa	auf	bur	daw	eek	feu	gip	hie	jak	kyu
aas	auk	bys	deb	een	fey	gis	hin	jap	la
aat	ava	cam	dee	ef	fid	git	ho	jar	lac
aba – Sack-like garment	ave	caw	def	eff	fil	gju	hoa	jee	lah
abb	aw	cay	dei	efs	fir	glyph	hoc	jeu	lam
aby	awa	cee	del	eft	fiz	glyphs	hod	jiz	lar
ach	awn	cel	dey	ehs	flysch	gnu	hoh	jo	las
act	ax	cep	di	*eik – Greasing liniment*	foh	goa	hoi	jor	lat
ad	ay	ch	dib	el	fon	goe	hon	jow	lav
ado	ays	cha	dit	eld	fou	gon	hoo	jud	law
ads	ayu	che	div	ell	foy	goo	hos	jus	lea
adz	ba	chi	do	els	fra	gos	hox	ka	led
ae	baa	cid	dob	elt	fro	gov	hoy	kae	lee
aft	bah	cig	doc	eme	fub	goy	htmn	kai	lei
aga	bam	cit	dod	emu	fud	gu	hub	kam	lek
ah	bel	cly	doh	ene	fug	gub	hue	kas	lep
aha	ben	col	doo	eng	fum	gue	hug	kat	les
ahs	bey	con	dop	ere	fy	gup	huh	kaw	leu
ai – S. American 3-toed sloth	bez	coo	dor	erf	gad	gur	hui	kay	lev
aia	bi	cop	dos	erg	gae	gus	hup	kea	lew
ail	bio	cor	dow	erk	gal	guv	hut	keb	lex
ain	bis	cos	dso	ern	gam	guy	hwyl	ked	ley
ais	biz	coz	dub	err	gan	gymp	hwyls	kef	lez
ake	bo	cru	dun	ers	gar	gymps	hye	keg	li
ala	boa	cud	duo	es	gat	gyny	*hyp – Hypochondria*		
alb	bod	cuz	dup	ess	gau	gyp	hyps	ken	lib
alp	boh	cwm	dux	est	ged	gyppy	ich	kep	lig
als	bok	cwms	dzo	eta	gee	gyps	id	ket	lin
alt	bon	da	ea	eth	gen	hae	ide	kex	lip
ami	bop	dae	ean	euk	geu	hah	ids	key	lis
ana	bor	dag	eas	euoi	gey	haj	iff	kif	lit
ane	bos	dah	eau	euoua	ghi	han	ifs	kir	lor
ani	bot	dak	ech	ewk	ghyll	hap	ins	ko	los
ann	bow	dal	eco	ewt	ghylls	haw	io	koa	lox
ar	bro	dan	ecu	ex	gi	hep	ion	kob	loy
arb	brrr	dap	edh	fa	gib	hes	ios	kon	lud
ard	bub	das	ee	fah	gid	het	ish	kop	lug
ars				fap	gie	hew	ism	kos	lum
ary				fas	gif	hex	iso	kow	lur
				faw	gio	hic	ita	ky	luv
				fet			jag	kye	lux

USEFUL WORDS cont.

luz lye lym lyms ma maa mac mae mag mak mal mar mas maw max meg mel mes meu mew mho mi mil

na nab nae nam nan nas nat ne neb ned nee nef nek nep nid nie nil nim nis nix noh nom nos

oda ods oe oes oh oho oi oke ole olm om oms ons oo oof ooh oom oon oop oor oos ope orc

pap par pas pax pec ped ph phi pho phs pi pia pic pir piu pix po poa poh poi pom pos pow

mim – *Modest and demure*

mir miz mna mo moa moe mog moi mon mor mot mou moy mu mun mus mux

nox noy nth nu nur nus ny nye nys ob oba obi obo obs oca och od

ord orf ors ort os ou ouk oup ova ow owt oy oye oys pa pah pam

poz pre prys psi psst pst puh pur pye pyx qat

qi – *A vital force in Taoism*

qis qua rad

rah raj ras rax ray re rec ree ref reh rem ren rep res ret rev rew rex rez rho rhy ria rin rit riz rob roc rok rom roo ruc rud rya rynd rynds sab sae sai sal sam

san sar saz scry sec sed seg sei sel sen set sez sh si sib sic sim ska sma sny soc sog soh sol son sos sot sou sov sox st sub sui suk sup suq sur sus swy sye

sylph sylphs synd synds syzygy ta tae tai taj tak tam tau taw tay te ted tef teg tel ten tes tew thymy ti tid tig til tim toc tod tor tryp tryps tui tum tut tux twa twp tye

tyg tymp tynd udo uds uey ufo

wat waw wem wen wex wey wha

yok yon yos yow yu yug yuk

ug – *Fear or dread*

ugh ugs uke uli um un uni uns ups ur urd ure ut ute uts utu uva vac vae van vas vau vee vid vin vly voe vol vor vug vum wae wap

wis wo wok won wop wos wot wox wud wus wye wyn wynd wynds wynn wynns wyns xi xis xu xylyl xylyls xyst xysts yah yaw yep yew yex ygo yin yo yod

yup yus zap zax zea zed zee zek zel zex zho zig ziz zo zoa zos zuz

Most obvious words have been omitted.

KNITTING ABBREVIATIONS

*	indicates a repeat
approx.	approximately
b	in back of stitch; bobble
beg	beginning
bh	button hole
bo	bind off; body gauge
col	color
con; cc	contrasting color
con	cast on
cont.	continue
dtr	double treble crochet
e	every
ea.	each
e(o)r	every (other) row
est	established
fol	following
g-st	garter stitch
kssb	knit slip stitch through back
m	make
mc	main color
mr	mark row
ms.	mark stitch
odl.	or desired length
p	purl
pat.	pattern
pfc.	present for Christmas
psso	pass slipped stitch(es) over
pu	pick up
r(h).	right (hand)
rem	remaining
rep	repeat
req.	required
rev	reverse
rnd	round
rs	right side
selv	selvedge
sk	skein
skp	slip, knit, psso
sl	slip
ssk	slip, slip, knit 2 tog
st(s)	stitch(es)
st st.	stockinette stitch
tbl	through the back loop
tfl	through the front loop
tog.	together
ws.	wrong side
x.	times
yb.	yarn back
yf.	yarn forward
yo	yarn over

ABRACADABRA

The word employed by so many second-rate conjurers has long had associations with magic and superstition. The first written example of *abracadabra* is thought to be in the poem *Praecepta de Medicina*, by the writer Q. Severus Sammonicus in the second century. When written in the triangular form shown opposite, and when worn around the neck, *abracadabra* was considered to have healing powers, perhaps

```
A B R A C A D A B R A
 A B R A C A D A B R
  A B R A C A D A B
   A B R A C A D A
    A B R A C A D
     A B R A C A
      A B R A C
       A B R A
        A B R
         A B
          A
```

because it repeated the letters ABRA – a possible reference to the Hebrew words signifying Father, Son, and Holy Spirit: *Ab, Ben* & *Ruach Acadosh*.

THE NINE MUSES

CLIO *history* · MELPOMENE *tragedy* · THALIA *comedy*
CALLIOPE *epic poetry* · URANIA *astronomy* · EUTERPE *flutes and music*
TERPSICHORE *dancing and lyric poetry*
POLYHYMNIA *mime and sacred poetry* · ERATO *love poetry*

The Nine Muses are the Greek goddesses of learning, arts, culture, and inspiration. They are the progeny of Zeus and Mnemosyne (memory), and were born in Pieria at the foot of Mount Olympus. For centuries the Muses have been worshipped and venerated for their patronage of music, art, drama, and poetry – not least by Plato, Aristotle, and Ptolemy I. Traditionally, those places dedicated to the greater glory of the Nine Muses were known as *mouseion*, from which we derive the word *museum*.

SOME MUSICAL TERMINOLOGY

Adagio .... slow	*Lontano* .... as from a distance
Affrettando ...... hurrying onwards	*Lusingando* .... caressingly
Agitati .... agitated	*Ma non troppo* .. but not too much
Allargando .... getting slower	*Mancando* .... dying away
Allegro .... fast, lively	*Martellato* .... hammered out
Andante .... walking pace	*Morendo* .... slowly dying away
Animato .... animated	*Nobilmente* .... nobly
Appassionato .... passionately	*Parlante* .... sung as spoken
Arpeggiare .... like a harp	*Passionato* .... passionately
Bravura .... boldness and spirit	*Patètico* .... with great feeling
Brio .... vigor	*Piacevole* .... agreeably
Con anima .... with feeling	*Pizzicato* .... plucked, picked
Deciso .... decisively, firmly	*Prestissimo* .... as fast as possible
Dolce .... sweetly, tenderly	*Rallentando* .... gradually slower
Dolcissimo ... very sweetly & gently	*Rigoroso* .... strictly, rigorous
Dolente .... sadly	*Risvegliato* .. increasingly animated
Energico .... with energy	*Ritardando* .... gradually held back
Forte-piano .... loud, then soft	*Scherzando* .... playful
Forzando .... sudden emphasis	*Slargando* .... gradually slower
Fugato .... in fugal style	*Smorzando* .... dying away
Grave .... slow and solemn	*Staccato* .... detached
Impetuoso .... impetuously	*Strepitoso* .... boisterously
Lacrimoso .... sadly, tearfully	*Suave* .... gentle, smooth
Largo .... slow and stately	*Tacet* .... silent
Legato .... smoothly	*Tempo primo* ...... at original speed
Leggiero .... nimble and delicate	*Teneramente* .... tenderly
L'istesso tempo ...... maintain speed	*Tranquillo* .... calmly

————————— PRESIDENTIAL SUCCESSION —————————

The succession of the President is covered by the Presidential Succession Act 1947, and the 25th Amendment to the Constitution 1967. If the President of the United States is incapacitated, dies, resigns, is for any reason unable to hold office, or is removed from office (impeached and convicted), then the office of President is assumed in the following order:

Vice President · Speaker of the House
President *Pro Tempore* of the Senate
Secretary of State · Secretary of the Treasury
Secretary of Defense · Attorney General · Secretary of the Interior
Secretary of Agriculture · Secretary of Commerce · Secretary of Labor
Secretary of Health and Human Services
Secretary of Housing and Urban Development
Secretary of Transportation · Secretary of Energy
Secretary of Education · Secretary of the Veterans' Affairs

[The succession assumes that each individual is qualified as specified by the Constitution: i.e. they must be at least 35 years old; a natural-born US citizen; and must have lived in the US for at least 14 years. Any individual who acts as President shall be entitled to be paid the Presidential salary.]

————————— TOP FIVE OSCAR WINNERS —————————

To date only three films have ever taken all of the 'top five' Academy Awards – Best Picture, Director, Actor, Actress, & Screenplay. They are:

YEAR	FILM	DIRECTOR
1934	*It Happened One Night*	Frank Capra
1975	*One Flew Over the Cuckoo's Nest*	Milos Forman
1991	*The Silence of the Lambs*	Jonathan Demme

————————— THE MASON-DIXON LINE —————————

The Mason-Dixon Line is the Southernmost boundary that divided Pennsylvania from Maryland. The Line was set at *c.*39º 42' 26" north by the two British surveyors Charles Mason and Jeremiah Dixon who marked out the land between 1773–7. Before the Civil War, the line represented the division between the Southern pro-slavery and the Northern free states. In common usage nowadays it represents the informal division between the North and the South. The Line is one of the possible etymological sources for the terms 'Dixie' and 'Dixieland'.

——————— BON MOTS OF DOROTHY PARKER ———————

Dorothy Rothschild Parker (1893–1967) was a poet, critic, satirist, and writer. Remembered today less for her formal writing than for her caustic wit, some of Parker's more memorable turns-of-phrase are quoted below:

Sorrow is tranquillity remembered in emotion.

That woman can speak eighteen languages and she can't say no in any of them.

Scratch a lover, and find a foe.

Men seldom make passes at girls who wear glasses.

You can lead a horticulture, but you can't make her think.

They sicken of the calm that know the storm.

Brevity is the soul of lingerie.

On Katharine Hepburn: She ran the whole gamut of emotions from A to B.

On being told President Coolidge was dead: How do they know?

Wit has truth in it; wisecracking is merely calisthenics with words.

This is not a novel to be tossed aside lightly. It should be thrown aside with great force.

If you want to know what God thinks of money, just look at the people he gave it to.

Her epitaph: Excuse my dust.

——————— PIG LATIN HAMLET ———————

Otay ebay, orway otnay otay ebay: atthay isway ethay estionquay:
Etherwhay 'istay oblernay inway ethay indmay otay uffersay
Ethay ingsslay andway arrowsway ofway outrageousway ortunefay,
Orway otay aketay armsway againstway away easay ofway oublestray,
Andway ybay opposingway endway emthay?

To be, or not to be: that is the question:
Whether 'tis nobler in the mind to suffer
The slings and arrows of outrageous fortune,
Or to take arms against a sea of troubles,
And by opposing end them?

——————— BRONTË SIBLINGS ———————

Charlotte (1816-55) · Emily (1818-48) · Anne (1820-49) · Branwell (1817-48)

—————————————— METRIC WIRE GAUGES ——————————————

The following table gives the metric equivalents for the British Standard Wire Gauge (SWG). Readers familiar with wire gauges will not need reminding of the importance of distinguishing between SWG and the other wire-gauges including: American Wire Gauge (AWG) [also known as Brown & Sharpe]; Birmingham Sheet & Hoop; Stubs; Stubs Steel; Stubs Iron (Birmingham Gauge); US standard plate; and Washburn & Moen.

STANDARD WIRE GAUGE	DIAMETER OF WIRE inch	cm						
0	.324	.823	15	.072	.183	33	.0100	.0254
1	.300	.762	16	.064	.163	34	.0092	.0234
2	.276	.701	17	.056	.142	35	.0084	.0213
3	.252	.640	18	.048	.122	36	.0076	.0193
4	.232	.589	19	.040	.102	37	.0068	.0173
5	.212	.538	20	.036	.0914	38	.0060	.0152
6	.192	.488	21	.032	.0813	39	.0052	.0132
7	.176	.447	22	.028	.0711	40	.0048	.0122
8	.160	.406	23	.024	.0610	41	.0044	.0112
9	.144	.366	24	.022	.0559	42	.0040	.0102
10	.128	.325	25	.020	.0508	43	.0036	.0091
11	.116	.295	26	.018	.0457	44	.0032	.0081
12	.104	.264	27	.0164	.0417	45	.0028	.0071
13	.092	.234	28	.0149	.0378	46	.0024	.0061
14	.080	.203	29	.0136	.0345	47	.0020	.0051
			30	.0124	.0315	48	.0016	.0041
			31	.0116	.0295	49	.0012	.0030
			32	.0108	.0274	50	.0010	.0025

—————————————— LUCASIAN PROFESSORS ——————————————

The Lucasian *Professorship of Mathematick* was endowed by Henry Lucas, MP for Cambridge University. On his death in December 1663, Lucas bequeathed land in his will to create an annual income of £100 to finance the chair. The Professorship received the ratification of Charles II in 1664.

1664–1669 . . . . Isaac Barrow[F]	1826–1828 . . . . Sir George Airy[P]
1669–1702 . . . . Sir Isaac Newton[P]	1828–1839 . . . . Charles Babbage[F]
1702–1710 . . . . William Whiston	1839–1849 . . . . Joshua King
1711–1739 . . . . Nicolas Saunderson[F]	1849–1903 . . . . . . Sir George Stokes[P]
1739–1760 . . . . John Colson[F]	1903–1932 . . . . . . Sir Joseph Larmor[V]
1760–1798 . . . . Edward Waring[F]	1932–1969 . . . . Paul Dirac[F]
1798–1820 . . . . Isaac Milner[F]	1969–1980 . . . . . Sir James Lighthill[V]
1820–1822 . . . . . Robert Woodhouse[F]	1980– . . . . Stephen Hawking[F]
1822–1826 . . . . Thomas Turton	Royal Society: [P]resident · [V]ice-President · [F]ellow

—MURDER METHODS IN MISS MARPLE NOVELS—

The following chart tabulates some of the murder techniques employed in the *Miss Marple* novels of Dame Agatha Christie. It excludes the short stories.

	gunshot	burning	head wound	strangling	falling	poison		
Murder at the Vicarage	▨						....	1930
The Body in the Library		▨	▨		▨		....	1942
The Moving Finger			▨		▨		....	1943
A Murder is Announced	▨			▨			....	1950
They Do It With Mirrors	▨			▨			....	1952
A Pocket Full of Rye				▨		▨	....	1953
4.50 From Paddington				▨		▨	....	1957
The Mirror Crack'd From Side to Side	▨					▨	....	1962
A Caribbean Mystery						▨	....	1964
At Bertram's Hotel	▨						....	1965
Nemesis			▨	▨	▨		....	1971
Sleeping Murder				▨			....	1976

COLOR SPECTRUM & MNEMONIC

Red *ichard* **O**range *f* **Y**ellow *ork* **G**reen *ave* **B**lue *attle* **I**ndigo *n* **V**iolet *ain*

CASTRATI

The Castrato voice (created by the removal of the testes of a young choirboy) was either soprano or alto, and it developed as the Castrato matured. Though never officially sanctioned by the Church, the practice of castration lasted in Europe from the mid 16th century until the 1870s. Famous Castrati include: SENESINO (*c.*1680–1759); FARINELLI (1705–82); MANZUOLI (1725–82); and the 'last castrato' MORESCHI (1858–1922), who entered the Sistine Chapel in 1883, and became conductor of the choir in 1898. Moreschi made seventeen recordings before he retired in 1913.

A FEW ANGLO-INDIAN WORDS

Pukka	.... first rate	*Chotta*	.... small
Chitty	.... letter, note or pass	*Pani*	.... water
Khak	.... dust (hence khaki)	*Sub chiz*	.... everything
Kutcha	.... opposite of *pukka*	*Jharan*	.... cloth, duster
Wallah	..... person, usually worker	*Peg*	.... a measure of drink

GEORGE WASHINGTON'S RULES

In his fourteenth or fifteenth year, the young George Washington kept a commonplace book he entitled *Forms of Writing*. Among other miscellaneous items, this book contained a list of a hundred and ten *Rules of Civility and Decent Behaviour in Company and Conversation*. Many writers, including Washington Irving, Dr J.M. Toner, and Moncure Conway, have discussed the possible source of these maxims, and it seems likely that they originate from the work of sixteenth century French Jesuits. A few of the Rules are quoted below, as Conway puts it, 'with the hope that they will do more than amuse the reader by their quaintness'.

1st   Every Action done in Company ought to be with Some Sign of Respect, to those that are Present.

2nd   When in Company, put not your hands to any Part of the Body not usually Discovered.

6th   Sleep not when others Speak, Sit not when others stand, Speak not when you should hold your Peace, walk not when others stop.

16th   Do not puff up the Cheeks, Loll not out the tongue rub the Hands, or beard, thrust out the lips, or bite them or keep the lips too open or too close.

19th   Let your Countenance be pleasant but in Serious Matters Somewhat grave.

22nd   Shew not yourself glad at the Misfortune of another though he were your enemy.

25th   Superfluous Complements and all Affectation of Ceremony are to be avoided, yet where due they are not to be Neglected.

38th   In visiting the Sick, do not Presently play the Physician if you be not Knowing therein.

44th   When a man does all he can though it Succeeds not well, blame not him that did it.

48th   Wherein you reprove Another be unblameable yourself; for example is more prevalent that Precepts.

54th   Play not the Peacock, looking everywhere about you, to See if you be well Dek't, if your shoes fit well if your Stockings Sit neatly, and Cloths handsomely.

56th   Associate yourself with Men of good Quality if you Esteem your own Reputation; for 'tis better to be alone than in bad Company.

60th   Be not immodest in urging your Friends to Discover a Secret.

71st   Gaze not at the marks or blemishes of Others and ask not how they came. What you may Speak in Secret to your Friend deliver not before others.

———— GEORGE WASHINGTON'S RULES cont. ————

77th Treat with men at fit Times about Business & Whisper not in the Company of Others.

80th Be not Tedious in Discourse or in reading unless you find the Company pleased therewith.

85th In Company of those of Higher Quality than yourself Speak not till you are ask'd a Question then Stand upright put of your Hat & Answer in a few words.

91st Make no Shew of taking great Delight in your Victuals, Feed not with Greediness; cut your Bread with a Knife, lean not on the Table, neither find fault with what you Eat.

107th If others talk at Table be attentive but talk not with Meat in your Mouth.

108th When you Speak of God or his Attributes, let it be seriously & with words of Reverence. Honour & obey your Natural Parents altho they be Poor.

109th Let your Recreations be Manful not Sinful.

110th Labour to keep alive in your Breast that Little Spark of Celestial fire called Conscience.

The exact wording of a few of the Rules has been lost as a result of damage to the manuscript by mice.

— CENTRAL CROSSINGS OF THE RIVER THAMES —

Kew · Chiswick · Barnes · Hammersmith · Putney · Wandsworth · Battersea · Albert · Chelsea · Vauxhall · Lambeth · Westminster · Hungerford Foot · Waterloo · Blackfriars · Millennium · Southwark · London · Tower · Rotherhithe Tunnel · Greenwich Foot Tunnel · Blackwall Tunnel

———— SOME COMPOUNDS ————

Testosterone............ $C_{19}H_{28}O_2$	Fool's Gold................... FeS_2
Asbestos .... $CaMg_3(SiO_3)_4$	Limestone................ $CaCO_3$
Aspirin.... $CH_3CO_2C_6H_4COOH$	Nitroglycerin.......... $H_5(NO_3)_3$
Vitamin A .... $C_{20}H_{29}OH$	Caffeine.............. $C_8H_{10}O_2N_4$
Clay.......... $H_2Al_2(SiO_4)_2 \cdot H_2O$	Saltpeter .... KNO_3
Camphor .... $C_{10}H_{16}O$	Adrenaline .... $C_9H_{13}NO_3$

---------------- ANATOLE'S DISHES ----------------

Anatole is the famous gourmet chef at Brinkley Court, the home of Bertie Wooster's favorite uncle and aunt: Tom and Dahlia Travers. Anatole's culinary creations are legendary, and the threat of never tasting them again is usually enough to induce Bertie to do his aunt's bidding in some burglarious enterprise. Scattered through the Jeeves & Wooster novels of P.G. Wodehouse, a few of these splendid dishes are tabulated below:

> *Velouté aux fleurs de courgette · Sylphides à la crème d'Ecrivisses*
> *Mignonette de poulet petit duc · Niege aux perles des Alpes*
> *Timbale de ris de veau Toulousaine · Points d'asperges à la Mistinguette*
> *Nonettes de poulet Agnès Sorel · Selle d'Agneau aux laitures à la Grecque*
> *Diablotins · Caviar Frais · Benedictins Blancs*

---------------- THE METALS OF ALCHEMY ----------------

Alchemy is the transmutation of base elements into precious metals such as silver and gold. The process has fascinated philosophers, scientists, clerics, and astrologers throughout time and across cultures. The metals usually linked with this (so far) fruitless search are shown below, along with the planets and deities that they are most commonly associated with.

> GOLD *Apollo, the Sun* · SILVER *Diana, the Moon* · TIN *Jupiter*
> QUICKSILVER *Mercury* · COPPER *Venus* · IRON *Mars* · LEAD *Saturn*

---------------- CLASSIFICATION OF ICEBERG SIZE ----------------

HEIGHT	NAME	LENGTH
meters above water		*meters*
<1	GROWLER	<5
1–4	BERGY BIT	5–14
5–15	SMALL	15–60
16–45	MEDIUM	61–120
46–75	LARGE	121–200
>75	VERY LARGE	>200

[The 'tip of the iceberg' is usually thought to be around 1/5th to 1/7th of its total size.]

---------------- GULLIVER'S TRAVELS ----------------

Lemuel Gulliver voyaged to Lilliput, Brobdingnag, Laputa, Balnibarbi, Luggnagg, Glubbdubdrib, Japan, and to the Land of the Houyhnhnms.

―――――――― SESQUIPEDALIAN ――――――――

Commonly cited as the longest word in English, the 1,185-character-long name for *Tobacco Mosaic Virus, Dahlemense Strain,* in all its absurdity, is:

*Acetylseryltyrosylsery
lisoleucylthreonylserylprolylserylg
lutaminylphenylalanylvalylphenylalanylle
ucylserylserylvalyltryptophylalanylaspartylprolyl
isoleucylglutamylleucylleucylasparaginylvalylcysteinyl
threonylserylserylleucylglycylasparaginylglutaminylphenyl
alanylglutaminylthreonylglutaminylglutaminylalanylarginy
lthreonylthreonylglutaminylvalylglutaminylglutaminylphenyla
lanylserylglutaminylvalyltryptophyllysylprolylphenylalanylprolylg
lutaminylserylthreonylvalylarginylphenylalanylprolylglycylasparty
lvalyltyrosyllysylvalyltyrosylarginylyrosylasparaginylalanylvalylleu
cylaspartylprolylleucylisoleucylthreonylalanylleucylleucylglycylthreo
nylphenylalanylaspartylthreonylarginylasparaginylarginylisoleucyli
soleucylglutamylvalylglutamylasparaginylglutaminylglutaminylse
rylprolylthreonylthreonylalanylglutamylthreonylleucylaspartylal
anylthreonylarginylarginylvalylaspartylaspartylalanylthreonyl
valylalanylisoleucylarginylserylalanylasparaginylisoleucylas
paraginylleucylvalylasparaginylglutamylleucylvalylargin
ylglycylthreonylglycylleucyltyrosylasparaginylglutam
inylasparaginylthreonylphenylalanylglutamyls
erylmethionylserylglycylleucylvalyltrypt
ophylthreonylserylalanylprolyl
alanylserine*

Other lovely long words include:

Pneumonoultramicroscopicsilicovolcanoconiosis
a disease caused by the inhalation of fine particles

Antitransubstantiationalist
one who doubts the validity of transubstantiation

Floccinaucinihilipilification
the estimation of a thing as worthless

Antidisestablishmentarianism
opposition of those who oppose the link between Church and State

Sesquipedalian is an interesting word in itself. Said to be coined by Horace, it is a term for words so polysyllabic that they seem 'a foot and a half long'.

CATTLE BRANDING

Cattle branding has a complex taxonomy, allowing the experienced eye to distinguish between a wide array of marks. There are, however, a few basic rules. The first is that brands are 'spoken' as they are read. For example, a diamond shape followed by the letter Q, would be called the *diamond-q* brand. And brands are read according to the following three conventions:

from left to right	from top to bottom	from outside in
QT *q-t*	**A** over **F** *a-f*	Ⓚ *circle-k*

Brands are constructed from letters, numbers, shapes, and symbols, most of which can be modified in a number of ways. For example, a character which is upside-down is *crazy;* a character which is back to front is *reverse;* a character with 'wings' is *flying,* and one with 'feet' is *walking.* (If the feet slope backwards, however, it is *dragging.*) A character rotated ninety degrees in either direction is *lazy.* A character written in a free-hand style is *running* and, if shown on a slant, is *tumbling.* (To avoid confusion, not all characters can be used in every way. For example, Ms and Ws cannot be *crazy,* and Xs cannot be *running.*) Below are just a few examples:

reverse-e lazy-f tumbling-t walking-a dragging-a flying-h crazy-r

To create unique brands, characters are combined with a wide variety of shapes and pictograms. Some are obvious (*box, diamond, circle, heart, moon, sun*), whereas others are more subtle. A short dash is a *bar,* but a long dash is a *rail.* Two long dashes are *two rails* but three become *stripes.* Half a diamond placed over a letter is a *half diamond,* but if the diamond is elongated, it becomes a *rafter.* A semi-circle above or below a character is a *quarter circle* (unless it touches the character, in which case the character is *swinging*). Furthermore, characters and shapes can be joined together to create more elegant designs (though they are read in the same way). Below are some examples to illustrate this vocabulary of branding:

Translation, from left to right: *box-walking-r · bar-b-q*
lazy-2-diamond · j-quarter-circle · tumbling -flying-h · swinging-reverse-p
diamond-6-rail · rafter-seven · slash-lazy-f · diamond-and-a-half

[*The term 'maverick' is commonly used to define free-thinkers and iconoclasts. It is derived from Samuel A. Maverick (1803–70), the Texan land baron and politician who refused to brand his calves. Unbranded (or motherless) cattle are still known as mavericks to this day.*]

SOME PRIME NUMBERS

2	61	149	239	347	443	563	659	773	887
3	67	151	241	349	449	569	661	787	907
5	71	157	251	353	457	571	673	797	911
7	73	163	257	359	461	577	677	809	919
11	79	167	263	367	463	587	683	811	929
13	83	173	269	373	467	593	691	821	937
17	89	179	271	379	479	599	701	823	941
19	97	181	277	383	487	601	709	827	947
23	101	191	281	389	491	607	719	829	953
29	103	193	283	397	499	613	727	839	967
31	107	197	293	401	503	617	733	853	971
37	109	199	307	409	509	619	739	857	977
41	113	211	311	419	521	631	743	859	983
43	127	223	313	421	523	641	751	863	991
47	131	227	317	431	541	643	757	877	997
53	137	229	331	433	547	647	761	881	1009
59	139	233	337	439	557	653	769	883	1013

BOOKS OF THE BIBLE

Old Testament · Genesis · Exodus · Leviticus · Numbers · Deuteronomy
Joshua · Judges · Ruth · First Book of Samuel · Second Book of Samuel
First Book of Kings · Second Book of Kings · First Book of Chronicles
Second Book of Chronicles · Ezra · Nehemiah · Esther · Job · Psalms
Proverbs · Ecclesiastes · The Song of Songs, Song of Solomon, Canticles
Isaiah · Jeremiah · Lamentations · Ezekiel · Daniel · Hosea · Joel · Amos
Obadiah · Jonah · Micah · Nahum · Habakkuk · Zephaniah · Haggai
Zechariah · Malachi · *New Testament* · Gospel According to St Matthew
Gospel According to St Mark · Gospel According to St Luke · Gospel
According to St John · Acts of the Apostles · Epistle to the Romans · First
Epistle to the Corinthians · Second Epistle to the Corinthians · Epistle to
the Galatians · Epistle to the Ephesians · Epistle to the Philippians
Epistle to the Colossians · First Epistle to the Thessalonians · Second
Epistle to the Thessalonians · First Epistle to Timothy · Second Epistle to
Timothy · Epistle to Titus · Epistle to Philemon · Epistle to the Hebrews
Epistle of James · First Epistle of Peter · Second Epistle of Peter · First
Epistle of John · Second Epistle of John · Third Epistle of John · Epistle
of Jude · Revelation, Apocalypse · *Apocrypha* · The First Book of Esdras
The Second Book of Esdras · Tobit · Judith · Rest of Esther · The Wisdom
of Solomon · Ecclesiasticus, Wisdom of Jesus the Son of Sirach · Baruch
Song of the Three Children · Susanna · Bel and the Dragon · Prayer of
Manasses · First Book of the Maccabees · Second Book of the Maccabees

—— SOCIAL ETIQUETTE AT WASHINGTON ——

In 1877, Mrs E.B. Duffey penned *The Ladies' and Gentlemen's Etiquette: a complete manual of the manners and dress of American Society.* Among chapters on courtship, card-playing, letter-writing, and conversation, Mrs Duffey devoted special attention to *Social Etiquette at Washington.* On the subject of Presidential protocol she made the following pronouncements:

Washington Etiquette

The wife of the Chief-Justice, and not the wife of the President, is the first lady in the land, and takes precedence of all others. She holds receptions and receives calls, but she alone is excluded from all duty of returning calls. The life of a lady in society at Washington is exceedingly onerous, and more especially so if she is the wife of any official. Next in rank comes the wife of the President.

Social Duties of the President

It is made the duty of the President to give several state dinners and official receptions during each session of Congress. Besides these, there are the general receptions, at which time the White House is open to the public and every citizen of the United States has a recognized right to pay his respects to the President.

Presidential Receptions

On the days of the regular 'levées' the doors of the White House are thrown open, and the world is indiscriminately invited to enter them. No 'court'-dress is required to make one presentable at this republican court, but everyone dresses according to his or her own means, taste, or fancy. The fashionable carriage- or walking-dress is seen side by side with the uncouth homespun and home-made of the backwoodsman and his wife. Neither are there any forms and ceremonies to be complied with in gaining admittance to the presidential presence. You enter, an official announces you, and you proceed directly to the President and his lady and pay your respects. They exchange a few words with you, and then you pass on to make room for the throng that is pressing behind you. You loiter about the rooms for a short time, chatting with acquaintances, or watching the shifting panorama of faces, and then you quietly go out, and the levée is ended for you.

Private Calls Upon the President

If anyone wishes to make a private call upon the President, he will find it necessary to secure the company and influence of some official or special friend of the President. Otherwise, though he will be readily admitted to the White House, he will probably fail in obtaining a personal interview.

Mrs E.B. Duffey was also author of the instructive (though seemingly contradictory) texts *What Women Should Know* and *No Sex in Education.*

HRH A.G. CARRICK

When, in 1987, His Royal Highness the Prince of Wales submitted one of his watercolors for inclusion in the Royal Academy's annual Summer Exhibition, the painting was entered and accepted under the pseudonym Arthur George Carrick. The painting was signed 'C/87'. The selection of this Royal pseudonym can be explained by examining the Prince of Wales' official title: His Royal Highness Prince Charles Philip Arthur George, Prince of Wales, KG, KT, OM, GCB, AK, QSO, PC, ADC, Earl of Chester, Duke of Cornwall, Duke of Rothesay, Earl of Carrick, Baron of Renfrew, Lord of the Isles and Prince and Great Steward of Scotland.

TWO DICE ODDS

number	permutations	betting odds
12		35/1
11		17/1
10		11/1
9		8/1
8		31/5
7		5/1
6		31/5
5		8/1
4		11/1
3		17/1
2		35/1

DIRECTORS OF THE F.B.I.

Since the creation of the Federal Bureau of Investigation by President Theodore Roosevelt in 1908, there have been sixteen Directors ([†]six of whom were acting appointees only). The Director of the F.B.I. is appointed by the President, and the position is ratified by the US Senate. The acronymic official motto of the F.B.I. is 'Fidelity, Bravery, Integrity'.

Stanley Finch 1908–12	Clarence M. Kelley 1973–8
A. Bruce Bielaski 1912–9	William H. Webster 1978–87
William E. Allen .... 1919[†]	John Otto .... 1987[†]
William J. Flynn 1919–21	William S. Sessions 1987–93
William J. Burns 1921–4	Floyd I. Clarke .... 1993[†]
J. Edgar Hoover 1924–72	Louis J. Freeh 1993–2001
L. Patrick Gray .... 1972–3[†]	Thomas J. Pickard .... 2001[†]
William D. Ruckelshaus .... 1973[†]	Robert S. Mueller III 2001–

———— SOME BONSAI TREE TERMINOLOGY ————

SOME STYLES		HEIGHT SPECIFICATIONS	
CHOKKAN	formal upright	MAME	< 7 cm
MOYOGI	informal upright	SHOHIN	7–20 cm
KENGAI	cascading form	KIFU	20–40 cm
ISHI SEKI	planted on rock	CHU	40–60 cm
HOKIDACHI	broom-like form	DAI	> 60 cm
SABAMIKI	split trunk		
KABUDACHI	multiple trunks		

[As defined by the 20th Grand View Bonsai Exhibition Nippon Bonsai Taikan-ten.]

———— COFFEE SHOP SLANG ————

Barista	expert espresso maker
Brevé	espresso with semi-skimmed milk
Cake in a Cup	double cream, double sugar
Con Panna	with cream
Crema	dense golden foam found only on good espresso
Demitasse	small espresso cup
Double	two shots of coffee
Double Cupping	two takeaway cups to protect hands
Double Fun	flavoring both coffee and milk
Drip	regular, filter coffee
Dry	foamed (not steamed) milk
Foamless	no foamed milk
Grande	large cup
Granita	Latte with frozen milk
Harmless	Skinny and No Fun
Latte	with milk
Lungo	a long pull of espresso
Macchiato	marked or spotted
No fun	decaffeinated
Quad	four shots of coffee
Short	small cup
Shot in the dark	a cup of Drip, with a shot of espresso
Skinny	semi-skimmed milk
Split	half caff, half decaff
Tall	medium cup
Triple	three shots of coffee
Wet	steamed (not foamed) milk
Whipless	no whipped cream
Wild	with whipped cream
With room	cup not completely filled
With wings	to go

———————DINING ABOARD THE TITANIC———————

FIRST CLASS DINNER MENU · 14 APRIL 1912

Hors D'oeuvre Variès · Oysters

Consommé Olga · Cream of Barley

Salmon, Mousseline Sauce, Cucumber

Filet Mignons Lili · Sauté of Chicken, Lyonnaise · Vegetable Marrow Farcie

Lamb, Mint Sauce
Roast Duckling, Apple Sauce
Sirloin of Beef, Chateâu Potatoes

Green Peas · Creamed Carrots · Boiled Rice · Parmentier & New Potatoes

Punch Romaine

Roast Squab & Cress · Cold Asparagus Vinaigrette
Pâté De Foie Gras · Celery

Waldorf Pudding · Peaches in Chartreuse Jelly
Chocolate & Vanilla Eclairs · French Ice Cream

THE TITANIC WAS LOADED WITH THE FOLLOWING PROVISIONS:

Bacon and ham . . . . 7,500 lbs	Oranges . . . . 80 boxes (36,000)
Coffee . . . . 2,200 lbs	Potatoes . . . . 40 tons
Flour . . . . 200 barrels	Poultry and game . . . . . . 25,000 lbs
Fresh asparagus . . . . . . 800 bundles	Rice, dried beans, &c . . 10,000 lbs
Fresh butter . . . . 6,000 lbs	Salt and dried fish . . . . 4,000 lbs
Fresh cream . . . . 1,200 qts	Sausages . . . . 2,500 lbs
Fresh eggs 40,000	Sugar . . . . 10,000 lbs
Fresh fish . . . . 11,000 lbs	Sweetbreads 1,000
Fresh green peas . . . . 2,250 lbs	Tea . . . . 800 lbs
Fresh meat . . . . 75,000 lbs	Cigars 8,000
Fresh milk . . . . 1,500 gals	Items of crockery 57,600
Grapefruit . . . . 50 boxes	Pieces of cutlery 44,000
Ice Cream . . . . 1,750 qts	Pieces of glassware 29,000
Jams and marmalades . . . 1,120 lbs	Beer and stout . . . . . 20,000 bottles
Lemons . . . . 50 boxes (16,000)	Mineral waters . . . . . 15,000 bottles
Lettuce . . . . 7,000 heads	Spirits . . . . 850 bottles
Onions . . . . 3,500 lbs	Wines . . . . 1,500 bottles

BLOOMSBURY

'Bloomsbury' is thought to derive from *Blemondisberi* – the 13th-century manor of William Blemond. The area of London named after it has no formal borders, but is commonly understood to be that enclosed *South* of Euston Road; *North* of New Oxford Street & High Holborn; *East* of Tottenham Court Road; and *West* of Gray's Inn Road. Apart from the British Museum and the University of London, the area is perhaps best known for the 'Bloomsbury Group': a loose association of writers, artists, and academics in the early 1900s. The Group's most notable members included: Leonard and Virginia Woolf, E.M. Forster, Roger Fry, Vanessa and Clive Bell, Lytton Strachey, J.M. Keynes, and Duncan Grant. Predating this famous group was the little known 'Bloomsbury Gang' – an influential Whig faction formed in 1765 by the 4th Duke of Bedford.

LOUIS BRAILLE

An accident in his father's workshop left Louis Braille (1809–52) blind at the age of four. Some seven years later, Braille met Charles Barbier, a soldier who had conceived a 'night writing' code. Realizing the potential for communication with the blind, Braille developed a simplified version:

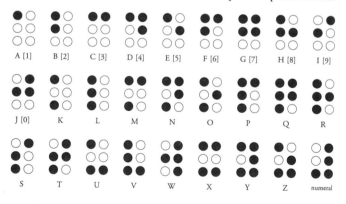

The numeral symbol indicates that the letters A–J are being used as digits.

Braille is based on the above 3x2 dot cells – although other cells exist for punctuation, abbreviations, and so on. A century and a half after Braille's death, his code has been adapted for almost every language, and is in use across the globe. To honor his unique creation, in 1952 Braille's body was exhumed and re-buried in the Panthéon alongside other French heroes.

— SOME WORDS FROM OTHER LANGUAGES —

MALAY · Quick! Go and fetch me the ornate *bamboo caddy*, or I will run *amok* in the *compound* wearing nothing but my *gingham sarong*.

ARABIC · The *admiral* in the *alcove*, while sitting on his *sequin sofa* dreaming of *harems*, should fear the *assassin* rather than seeking solace in the *alchemy* of *alcohol*.

IRISH GAELIC · Don't give me any more of your *Tory blarney* about the *banshee* wearing *brogues*, or I'll get that *colleen* to smash your *poteen* to *smithereens*.

JAPANESE · Only a *tycoon* or a *mikado* would have a *yen* to recline on his *futon* eating *sushi* with a *geisha*, while betting on *judo*.

ALEUT INUIT · My *anorak* is too cold for a *kayak* expedition to the *igloo*. Bring me that *parka* instead.

FARSI/PERSIAN · This *talc bazaar* has everything! Just one *kiosk* alone sells *lilac tiaras*, and *azure shawls*.

SANSKRIT · The *pundit* and his *guru* were repeating their *mantra*, hoping for *nirvana*, when some fool ruined their *karma*, chipping the *crimson lacquer* on the *chintz*.

TURKISH · Oh! *Effendi!* I really must apologize for spilling *coffee* over your *kilim*, and dripping *yogurt* over your *turquoise divan*.

CZECH · Fetch the *howitzer!* Some fool's armed the *robot* with a *pistol*.

AFRIKAANS · The *commandos* love nothing more than to *trek* across the *veldt* in search of *wildebeest*.

SWEDISH · The *ombudsman* was dazzled by the harsh *tungsten* light.

WELSH · Wrap that *corgi* in *flannel* and hide him in the *coracle*.

PORTUGUESE · All this *palaver* simply because the *albino albatross* doesn't have a taste for *marmalade*.

NORWEGIAN · It was an error to let the *lemming ski* in the *slalom*.

HUNGARIAN · Get the *saber* from the *coach!* The *hussar* has overdone the *paprika* and ruined my *goulash*.

ICELANDIC · A *saga* about a *geyser?*

SCOTTISH GAELIC · 'Toss the *caber* from the *glen* over the *loch*' is an absurd *slogan* if all you want to do is sell *plaid trousers* to tourists.

TAGALOG · Look over there. Is that a *ylang-ylang* in the *boondock?*

AZTEC · I'm not eating *avocado* with *chili* sauce, or *tomato* with *chocolate*. Feed it all to the *coyote!*

RUSSIAN · The *commissar* orders a *mammoth samovar* of *vodka* to be dispatched to the *balalaika* player.

NORSE · *Balderdash*, you *oaf!* I am so *angry*. If I get an *inkling* you are *flaunting* the *dregs* of your talent, I will cover your *vole* in *glitter*.

COURT JESTERS

Dr Doran, in his 1850 *The History of Court Fools,* gives an utterly exhaustive account of licensed and unlicensed court fools, jesters, and mirthmen throughout the ages. The following list is a very brief selection:

ADELSBURN . . . . Jester to George I
'CARDINAL' SOGLIA . . . . Jester to Pope Gregory XVI
MERRY ANDREW . . . . Physician to Henry VIII, and unlicensed fool
ABGELY . . . . Fool to Louis XIV; the last licensed fool in France
ROSEN . . . . Fool to Emperor Maximilian I
BERDIC . . . . *Joculacator* to William the Conqueror
COLQUHOUN . . . . Jester to the court of Mary Queen of Scots
LONGELY . . . . Jester to Louis XIII
PATCHE . . . . Cardinal Wolsey's Jester, presented to Henry VIII
DA'GONET . . . . Jester to King Arthur, who later knighted him
PATISON . . . . Jester to Sir Thomas More
WILL SOMERS . . . . Court Jester to Henry VIII at Hampton Court
YORICK . . . . Jester to the Court of Denmark
AKSAKOFF . . . . Fool to Czarina Elizabeth of Russia

'Better a witty fool than a foolish wit' — QUINAPALUS

OSCAR WILDE'S PARADOXES

Nowadays, all the married men live like bachelors, and all the bachelors like married men.

I can believe anything provided it is incredible.

It is only the modern that ever becomes old-fashioned.

All women become like their mothers. That is their tragedy. No man does. That's his.

I must decline your invitation owing to a subsequent engagement.

I can resist everything except temptation.

I love acting. It is so much more real than life.

Those whom the Gods love grow young.

The way to get rid of temptation is to yield to it.

He hadn't a single redeeming vice.

Skepticism is the beginning of Faith.

A man cannot be too careful in the choice of his enemies.

There is only one thing in the world worse than being talked about, and that is not being talked about.

A true friend stabs you in the front.

A FEW CONTRADICTORY PROVERBS

Beware of Greeks bearing gifts	*Don't look a gift horse in the mouth*
Many hands make light work	*Too many cooks spoil the broth*
No fool like an old fool	*With age comes wisdom*
Tomorrow's another day	*Tomorrow never comes*
Two heads are better than one	*Two of a trade never agree*
Great minds think alike	*Idiots seldom differ*
Fools rush in where angels fear to tread	*He who hesitates is lost*
Absence makes the heart grow fonder	*Out of sight, out of mind*
The tailor maketh the man	*Never judge a book by its cover*
You're never too old to learn	*You can't teach an old dog new tricks*
Familiarity breeds contempt	*Better the devil you know*
The more the merrier	*Two's company, three's a crowd*

CAFFEINE

Caffeine is perhaps the most widely used psychoactive drug in the world. A basic purine alkaloid, caffeine is readily soluble in hot water, and has a melting point of 235°C. Depending on strength and brew, 150ml of coffee can contain between 30–180mg of caffeine; 360ml of cola contains between 30–60mg.

WAR CRIES OF SOME SCOTTISH CLANS

Clan	*War Cry*
BUCHANAN	*Clar Innis*
CAMERON	*Chlanna nan con thigibh a so 's gheibh sibh feòil*[†]
SUTHERLAND	*Ceann na Drochaide Bige*
MACDONALD OF CLANRANALD	*Dh' aindeòin co theireadh e*
COLQUHOUN	*Cnoc Ealachain*
DOUGLAS FAMILY	*A Douglas! A Douglas!*
MACGREGOR	*Ard Choille*
FARQUHARSON	*Càrn na cuimhne*
MENZIES	*Geal is Dearg a suas*
FERGUSON	*Clannfearghuis gu brath*
FORBES	*Lònach*

[†] Translates as: *Sons of the hounds come here and get flesh*

———————— MRS BEETON'S KITCHEN MAXIMS————————

In *Everyday Cookery,* Isabella Beeton (1837–65) presents her list of culinary maxims. Beeton claims that 'if the novice will commit them to memory, she will have before her the fundamental truths of the art of cookery'.

There is no work like early work.

A good manager looks ahead.

Clear as you go. Muddle makes more muddle.

Not to wash plates and dishes soon after using makes more work.

Spare neither borax nor hot water in washing-up greasy articles.

Dirty saucepans filled with hot water begin to clean themselves.

Wash well a saucepan, but clean a frying-pan with a piece of bread.

Never put the [bone] handles of knives into hot water.

Thrust an oniony knife into the earth to take away the smell.

Search for the insects in greens *before* putting them in to soak.

Green vegetables should be boiled fast with the lid off.

Bread or vegetables left in stock turn it sour.

Roast meat should start in a hot oven.

When pastry comes out of the oven, meat may go in.

Fish boiled should be done slowly, with a little vinegar added.

A spoonful of vinegar will set a poached egg.

Water boils when it gallops, oil when it is still.

A stew boiled, is a stew spoiled.

Melt a teaspoonful of fat in a frying-pan before adding bacon.

Put spare crusts in the oven to grate for breadcrumbs.

Make mint sauce two hours before serving it.

Scum, as it rises in boiling, should be taken off.

No more water than is needed for gravy should be put in the pan.

Salt brings out flavors.

When using ketchup, be sparing with salt.

One egg, beaten well, is worth two not beaten.

Make the tea directly the water boils.

Draw fresh water for the kettle to boil for tea, cocoa, or coffee.

THE STAR-SPANGLED BANNER

Oh, say can you see, by the dawn's early light
What so proudly we hailed at the twilight's last gleaming?
Whose broad stripes and bright stars, thro' the perilous fight,
O'er the ramparts we watched, were so gallantly streaming.
And the rocket's red glare, the bombs bursting in air,
Gave proof through the night that our flag was still there.
Oh, say does that star-spangled banner yet wave
O'er the land of the free and the home of the brave?

On the shore dimly seen, thro' the mists of the deep,
Where the foe's haughty host in dread silence reposes,
What is that which the breeze, o'er the towering steep,
As it fitfully blows, half conceals, half discloses?
Now it catches the gleam of the morning's first beam,
In full glory reflected, now shines on the stream:
'Tis the star-spangled banner! Oh, long may it wave
O'er the land of the free and the home of the brave.

And where is that band who so vauntingly swore
That the havoc of war and the battle's confusion,
A home and a country should leave us no more?
Their blood has wash'd out their foul footstep's pollution.
No refuge could save the hireling and slave
From the terror of flight or the gloom of the grave,
And the star-spangled banner in triumph doth wave
O'er the land of the free and the home of the brave.

Oh, thus be it ever when free men shall stand,
Between their loved homes and the war's desolation!
Blest with vict'ry and peace, may the heav'n-rescued land
Praise the Power that has made and preserved us as a nation.
Then conquer we must, when our cause it is just,
And this be our motto: "In God is our trust".
And the star-spangled banner in triumph shall wave
O'er the land of the free and the home of the brave.

Written by *Francis Scott Key, 14 September 1814* · Tune *Anacreon in Heaven*

DEADLY SINS & CARDINAL VIRTUES

SINS — Pride · Greed · Lust · Envy · Gluttony · Anger · Sloth
VIRTUES — Prudence · Justice · Temperance · Fortitude

SPECIFICATIONS

— BOOK —

Paper.........................Clarion 55lb, 364ppi, cream white shade
Printing plates......................................Kodak Thermal CTP
Ink (text)..Heat set
Printing press (cover)...........................Heidelberg 6 Unit Press
Printing press (text)...Harris M110
Fold, gather, and trim..................................Kolbus Machine
Case making.......................................Sheridan Casemaker

— TYPESETTING —

Body .... *Adobe Garamond*	Dotted tabs.................... 6pt
Body font size............... 8.5pt	Weight of most lines 0.2pt
Baseline grid 9.51pt	Between title & text 9.51pt
Title........ *Old Style Bold Outline*	Paper-size .... 186 x 115mm
Title font size.................. 8pt	Paper-size ratio............ 1:1.61
Small Caps.................... 85%	Golden ratio 1:1.61
Copyright page font size 7pt	Bottom margin 20mm
Page numbering............... 8pt	Other margins 15mm

— FONT HISTORY —

Adobe Garamond was drawn by Robert Slimbach, and issued by Adobe Systems Inc. in 1989. The typeface is based upon the original designs and matrices of Claude Garamond (*c.*1490–1561), the legendary French printer, publisher, and designer. Claude Garamond was sceptical about linking roman and italic type, and consequently the italics of *Adobe Garamond* are based on the work of Robert Granjon (*c.*1513–90). Many designers and foundries have issued their own versions of *Garamond*, but Slimbach's Adobe font is perhaps the most elegant, versatile, and visually pleasing.

The designer of *Monotype Old Style Bold Outline*, also issued by Adobe, is not known. However, Old Style fonts are thought to date back to the 1860s, and some credit the work of Alexander Phemister (*c.*1829–94) who was employed at the Edinburgh foundry Miller & Richard. Old Style represented a break from the traditional look of Caslon, tending as it does towards shorter ascenders and descenders, and more elegant, simple serifs.

— MISCELLANEOUS —

Number of words 39,447
Library of choice...........................The British Library, London
% of F.B.I. Directors called William 37.5%
Favourite San Francisco cable-car line ....Powell–Hyde
Number of translations from 'arse' (UK) to 'ass' (US).................... 3
Quantity of beauty required to launch a single ship......... 1 Millihelen

───────── VARIATIONS & DISPUTATIONS ─────────

The research of this book has shown the actual fluidity of what might be thought hard fact. Below are just a few of the myriad disputes, variations, and possible inaccuracies encountered across the many sources consulted.

[*A letter after the page number indicates which of the entries on that page is referred to.*]

10d........... Shoelace length will vary depending on the style of shoe.
14 & 15 .... Some entries are tentative or the subject of debate.
18b................ Dates of line opening may not mean the entire line.
19 .. Unofficial films *(Casino Royale, Never Say Never Again)* are omitted.
24a.......... The description of some Amendments has been simplified.
26d...... Definition and enforcement of compulsory voting vary widely.
30a........................ Accepted ballistic missile ranges vary slightly.
34b .... 'Brunette' includes all dark hair; 'Redheaded' is subjective.
36a........................ The Riot Act 1714 came into force in 1715.
42b .... Layer heights are approximate, and vary around the globe.
46c ... Saints are usually credited with influence in a number of spheres.
51 ... Wide variations exist: male to female? formal? informal? phonetic?
54 .... Some colleges have a number of fight songs.
56a..... There are a wide number variant dimensions for nearly all sizes.
59a .. The layout of some hedges and culs-de-sac has changed over time.
60b........ Club-name variations exist: e.g. some called a Spoon a Baffy.
62a ... Over the years, *many* variations of this hierarchy have been given.
66c .... Various spellings exist. E.g. Caspar as Gaspar or Kaspar.
70b................................... Alecto: sometimes spelled Allecto.
75b .... Alternate spellings exist across editions.
76a... Israel's capability is disputed; other states are developing weapons.
78a ..... Relationship between Richter & Mercalli scales is approximate.
79 .... *The Irish Code Duello* is often erroneously quoted as 1877.
80...... Lady Jane Grey's status is disputed; House and Line names differ.
87c.... Some state Noble Gases as Group 18, or VIIIa of Periodic Table.
93a .... Various spellings exist for Haydn's Symphony No. 48.
105a... The historical definition of Belgian has been loosely interpreted.
107 .... Some positioning (e.g. River Phlegethon) is tentative.
119b....................... Savoy Court is off Strand, not 'The Strand'.
120–2....... Some entries (e.g. death penalty) are tentative & complex.
131a.... The characteristics of the Muses have been variously attributed.
132c............. Line co-ordinates are rough, and vary between sources.
138a....................... Menu spellings are those of P.G. Wodehouse.
143b .... 35 to 1 is taken as equivalent to 1 in 36.
145 .... Menu spelling has been taken verbatim from the original.
151a........... Subtle differences of punctuation exist between versions.

Corrections or suggestions may be emailed to: usa@miscellanies.info

INDEX

'I proposed to bring a bill into Parliament to deprive

an author who publishes a book without an index of the

privilege of copyright, and, moreover to subject him

for his offence to a pecuniary penalty.'

— LORD JOHN CAMPBELL

A FOR 'ORSES – BRONTË SIBLINGS

'There is nothing, Sir, too little for so little a creature as man.

It is by studying little things that we attain the great art of

having as little misery and as much happiness as possible.'

— SAMUEL JOHNSON